Christian Leadership

CHRISTIAN LEADERSHIP

BRUCE P. POWERS

Broadman Press
Nashville, Tennessee

4232–27
ISBN: 0–8054–3227–2

Dewey Decimal Classification: 301.15
Subject heading: LEADERSHIP

Library of Congress Catalog Card Number: 78–72841
Printed in the United States of America

Preface

What does it take to be a successful Christian leader? How might I be more useful to God and at the same time gain a greater sense of satisfaction from what I do? These questions have bothered me off and on for years.

Always I thought the answers would come in a rather specific, well-defined form so that I could learn how to be a successful Christian leader. Every time I thought I had found *the* answers, however, disappointment soon followed as some part of my newfound system failed.

Yes, I studied about leadership—authoritarian, laissez-faire, democratic, paternalistic, trait theory, great-person theory, and such—and went through many, many leadership books and manuals that describe how to administer church programs, list skills needed by a leader, tell how to lead a group, and even outline steps to effective leadership. And I am sure each experience was helpful in some way, because in the process of searching, I gradually came to understand what Christian leadership is all about.

I realized that the object of my search—how to be an effective Christian leader—was not to be found; at least it was not to be found in the form for which I was seeking. What I did discover was that the key to being an effective Christian leader is not so much in knowing a formula or acting in a particular way as it is in adopting a life-style based on certain principles.

These principles are process oriented. That is they do not provide answers, just guidelines for action. And, herein, was my answer: Effective Christian leadership is not so much a goal to be achieved as it is a means, or a life-style, that must be developed. It is a way of living that finds great variety in expression yet always focuses on bringing Christians into a maturing relationship with Jesus Christ. This involves growing personally and helping others to grow into all that they are capable of becoming, to the measure of the stature of the fullness of Christ (see Eph. 4:13, RSV).

These basic principles, and their meaning for the Christian leader, are described in this book not to provide *the* answer to Christian leadership but to help fellow strugglers in their process of growing toward maturity in Jesus Christ.

I am convinced that effective Christian leaders are those who, like their Lord, seek to enable others to experience life more abundantly (see John 10:10). Hence, I have chosen the term "life-giving leadership" to express the principles, practices, and intent of the approach to leadership described.

This book is designed with individual and group-learning activities in appropriate places so that you might experience firsthand some of the experiences underlying life-giving leadership. If you prefer to read straight through the book or to skip certain learning activities, simply pass over the sections indicated. Let me encourage you, however, to avoid the temptation of learning *about* life-giving leadership. To know is not to do in this case; you must personalize the concept, principles, and the techniques involved and commit yourself to a life-style. Herein lies the difference between those who would be first among many, receiving glory through leadership and those who would be servant of many, giving *life* through leadership.

Contents

1.
A New Concept
in Leadership

Life-giving leadership defies all the traditional concepts of what being a leader is all about. It is what might be termed eclectic in style, since a life-giving leader may at times appear authoritarian and at other times overly democratic. The life-giving leader is a person for all seasons, adjusting as the demands of a situation change. However, while leadership techniques and methods may vary, there is much beneath the surface that is unchanging.

Basic Values

Life-giving leadership is based on commitments in three interdependent areas: ministry, mission, and relationship. Only as a person develops an understanding of and commitment to these areas can he come to understand the principles and implications of life-giving leadership.

A Commitment to Ministry

Great leaders customarily exercise authority over others. But Jesus said that his followers must adopt different values: Whoever would be a leader must also be a servant (see Matt. 20:26).

Thus, basic to life-giving leadership are Jesus' teachings regarding the role of a Christian leader as minister, that is, he is *to serve.*

As a Christian leads he must discover and practice ways of serving those with whom he works. This is the first principle of life-giving leadership. However, it is not sufficient by itself.

A Commitment to Mission

The second principle relates to the intent of one's ministry. All leadership efforts are focused on a purpose. For the life-giving leader, however, purpose must not be tied up in seeking profit or public acclaim but in pursuing the same task pursued by Jesus: helping people to become all that they can become under God. Or as it is said so beautifully in Ephesians 4:13: "Until we all attain to the unity of the faith and of the knowledge of the Son of God, to mature manhood, to the measure of the stature of the fullness of Christ" (RSV).

This mission must be goal oriented and process oriented. That is, bringing mankind to a saving faith in Jesus Christ is only the first part of the mission. To grow fellow Christians toward full maturity is the complementing part of the mission that reinforces and provides additional resources to accomplish the first part. Thus the process becomes an integral part along with the goal in the mission of life-giving leaders.

A Commitment to Relationship

The third principle in life-giving leadership is that it is dependent on close, personal relationships with God and with fellow believers.

Life-giving leaders cannot function effectively in isolation. They are dependent on a personal relationship with God. As a part of this relationship they have the responsibility and the freedom to develop and exercise God-given talents. These leaders also must be part of a loving, caring, supportive body of believers in which they may develop and use their talents to serve others.

Thus the commitment to relationship becomes the foundation for a Christian community in which one is encouraged and supported as he pursues ministry and mission. It is such an environment that is nurturing ground for life-giving leaders.

Three principles, all necessary, and when interrelated, become the simple commitments that undergird a fascinating, life-changing approach to Christian leadership.

Action and Reaction

How are these three principles interrelated? How are they put into practice? Life-giving leadership is dependent on mastering some action and reaction behavior patterns that enable a person to determine (1) the type of leadership behavior needed in a particular situation and/or (2) the type of behavior to elicit from others to create the greatest potential for growth of those involved.

Here are descriptions of the action-reaction pattern in two significant areas.

Concern for Personhood

In Figure 1 is a continuum between low concern for personhood and high concern for personhood. Every leadership action can be located somewhere on this line depending on the leader's level of concern for the other person or other people involved. High concern implies great caring, concern, and love for others on the part of the leader. Low concern implies little or no caring, concern, or love for others.

Leadership actions related to concern for personhood tend

similar response

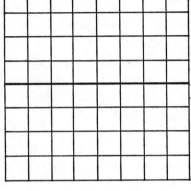

LOW   HIGH
CONCERN   CONCERN
FOR   FOR
PERSONHOOD   PERSONHOOD

Figure 1

to elicit a *similar* response on the part of others. For example, if a teacher exhibits low caring for those she teaches, her students will tend to react similarly with low caring for her and even for others. On the other hand, a parent who consistently exhibits high concern for a child's personhood tends to produce a child who has a healthy self-concept and places high value on the worth of persons in general.

Control of Others

The second area may also be depicted on a continuum as in Figure 2. At the extreme, high control of others is authoritarian leadership: Others are told what to do, how to do it, and when. There is little opportunity for individual decision-making or disagreement; people just follow the leader. An example of a leader who exerts this high degree of control is a military officer.

A less extreme example would be a pastor who is the final authority on all matters in his church. This person might be

HIGH **CONTROL OF OTHERS**
(Authoritarian behavior)

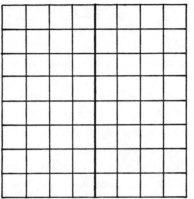

opposit
response

LOW **CONTROL OF OTHERS**
(Submissive behavior)

Figure 2

an *ex officio* member of all church committees and be consulted for his desires related to all significant decisions. The church in business meeting would always reflect the stance of the pastor.

Low control of others at the extreme represents a laissez-faire or submissive style of leadership in which the leader essentially takes a hands-off approach. His basic concern is to preserve harmony, letting others work at their own speed and initiative. An example of this leadership behavior is the stereotype of a husband who says to his wife, "Whatever you say, dear." A less extreme example is the group leader who avoids tension. He floats with the prevailing wishes of members and generally gravitates to the power position, staying in the background if possible.

Whereas leadership actions related to concern for person-hood elicit a *similar* response on the part of others, actions related to control of others tend to elicit the *opposite* response. In other words, if a leader consistently practices high control of others, he will tend to produce submissive followers, people who are indecisive and need to be told what, how, and when to do things.

A submissive or laissez-faire person, conversely, would tend to elicit a controlling form of behavior in others.

To assist in understanding the control aspect of leadership, let's consider a case study involving a relationship with which we are all familiar, mother and daughter.

Jane's mother was in a conference I was leading when discussing this topic. Toward the end of the session she asked if she could share something which I've recreated here:

> My daughter Jane was married several months ago. She and her husband seem to be doing quite well establishing their home; however every week or so my daughter calls to get my advice regarding things she should do. I've appreciated her continuing desire for my ideas and opinions and have gladly helped her.
>
> I've become disturbed tonight because, perhaps, the pleasure I gain from her continuing dependence on me might be unhealthy in the long run. As I look back, she was always very dependent so I ended up making most of her decisions for her, even up until she left home for good. Now I'm realizing that I may have produced a child who is overly dependent and submissive.

In talking with Jane's mother later she described how Jane had grown up a perfectly behaved, only child. Since her husband traveled extensively, she was the primary decision-maker and disciplinarian. She and Jane became overly dependent on each other, and she apparently sought to relive much of her life through her daughter. Jane seemed to enjoy the security that came as her mother selected her clothes and provided all the help needed with homework. Throughout high school and college, every time Jane needed help she could count on her mother.

When Jane became engaged, it was to the son of lifelong family friends. Her mother helped them every step of the way as they prepared for their life together. It was only natural for Jane, in the face of a problem, to turn to her mother, even after marriage. This had become her normal pattern of behavior reinforced by much success.

What happened in this situation was that Jane never quite left the dependency stage of early life. She did not move—nor was she encouraged to move—toward independence. Her principle leader did not help her develop discriminatory and problem-solving skills necessary for self-reliance. Values so important to character and behavior were probably adopted without question rather than evaluated, adapted, and freely chosen.

Jane's mother may have thought she was turning out a model child. What she didn't know was that her example of independent action and authoritative behavior would develop the *opposite* type of behavior in her daughter.

The Interrelationships

Now, let's see how these two patterns of action-reaction relate. In Figure 3, they are shown together.

Let's use the example of a pastor who has been at an old, established church for twenty-five years. As in the example given earlier he is an *ex officio* member of all committees, and all major decisions are checked through him. The staff, most major church leaders, and the congregation for the most part, wait on his lead in all church matters. At the same time he is a very loving, caring person who shows a high degree of

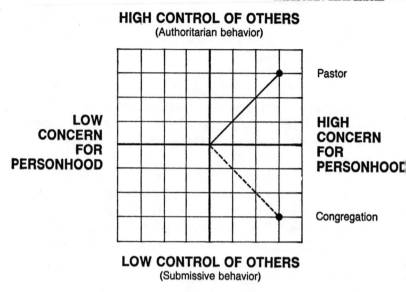

Figure 3

concern in his relations with his congregation. By using this information we can predict the behavior that will be elicited generally and the type of people that will be produced based on an extended relationship. The high control of others will tend to elicit the *opposite* response, submissive behavior, on the part of the congregation. The high concern for personhood will tend to elicit a *similar* response. Note in Figure 3 that the solid line locates the leadership behavior while the broken line indicates the behavior that would be expected in others.

This pastor would probably be greatly loved and appreciated for his dynamic leadership through the years. But what type of people would be produced? And what would happen when he left the church?

Some Considerations

Now let's deal with several points that seem to contradict the action-reaction pattern. What about exceptions to the pattern described? If you noticed, the word *tends* was used quite often. It was used deliberately because although the pattern described is basic, exceptions are numerous for any variety of reasons. The reasons aren't pertinent, but the result of exceptions is important: Whenever the action-reaction pattern is not followed, the result is tension which may be expressed in any number of ways such as through arguing, complaining, or decreased support of common goals.

In the example of the beloved pastor, anyone who did not respond in a caring, submissive manner would feel tension. This tension might be very slight such as could be handled by rationalization or a few hostile remarks now and then. But what if a church member had strong commitments that differed from those of the pastor, and he was not willing to be submissive to the pastor's leadership? The result: tension, perhaps at a very high level.

Tension can be healthy or destructive in life-giving leadership. At its worst, it becomes a disruptive and divisive factor. The life-giving leader must understand the role of tension and how to use it effectively; consequently, guidance is provided in subsequent chapters.

Another point is that few leaders are as consistent in style as the examples used. In one instance a person might seem extremely controlling and in another appear to be very freeing. At times a leader may exhibit extreme concern and in another case seem to be rather callous in comparison. While every action does tend to elicit the response described, it is the pattern of leadership-behavior established during extended relationships that tends to develop and grow people according to the action-reaction principle.

The last point relates to the interaction between a leader and others. While the action-reaction principle was described from a leadership perspective, it is a general principle; that is, it works both ways. Others can elicit behavior in the leader according to the same pattern. Everything that has been described happens all the time whether or not people understand the process. The life-giving leader, because of circumstance or knowledge, uses the process as a means for growing people, helping them to experience life in a more meaningful way.

2.
Relating to Others

While most leadership theories give primary emphasis to the role of the leader, life-giving leadership balances this emphasis with a concern for the role of those who are affected by the leader's actions.

Leadership as Perceived by Others

In the previous chapter, I described how a leader affects the lives of others. On first reading, it probably seemed simple enough for a person with a commitment to mission, ministry, and relationship to become an effective Christian leader. But what is often overlooked is that the leader is only one part of any situation. And frequently success is determined not so much by what the leader actually does as by how the leader and his actions are *perceived* by others. For example, if a leader's actions are perceived as manipulation, no matter how noble his intentions might be, it is this perception that determines the response of those he is seeking to lead.

Think with me back to the example in the previous chapter of the pastor who was high in control of others and high in concern for personhood. Through his leadership he had produced a basically dependent yet caring, concerned congregation. Let's say this pastor retired and the next pastor came with a different approach to leadership. He told committees that since they were given their guidelines by the church, that they should function without him as an ex officio member. Also, he insisted that the church function democratically in planning for the budget and in setting church goals. He felt the pastor should be primarily a guide and not the chief decision-maker.

In this case, the new pastor's intentions would be good, but his leadership would be perceived by many as weak or indecisive. The immediate result would be a high level of tension on the part of many, as can be determined by comparing the diagrams in Figure 4.

Tension would be produced, according to the action-reaction diagram on the bottom of page 23, because the new pastor and the congregation could not both be in the same quadrant. When a pastor's actions are interpreted as submissive or low in control of others, and the congregation has grown to be submissive to pastoral leadership, tension is the natural result. Tension would develop also if the new pastor did not exhibit a high level of concern and caring. The congregation, being high in concern for others, would expect the pastor to share this concern.

If your response resembles mine when I first understood this action-reaction pattern, you are probably amazed at its simplicity and yet perplexed by its implications. It is simple to understand and predict actions, but very perplexing when you realize that the implications are confusing and even disturbing. For instance, is leadership just a series of actions and reactions? Is it a building up and alleviating of tensions? Is leadership basically a control or be-controlled situation? What should the stance of the Christian leader be?

HIGH CONTROL OF OTHERS
(Authoritarian behavior)

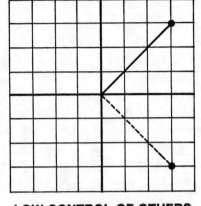

LOW
CONCERN
FOR
PERSONHOOD

HIGH
CONCERN
FOR
PERSONHOOD

Former
pastor

Congregation

LOW CONTROL OF OTHERS
(Submissive behavior)

HIGH CONTROL OF OTHERS
(Authoritarian behavior)

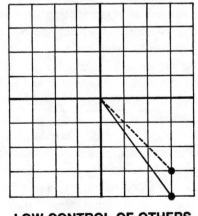

LOW
CONCERN
FOR
PERSONHOOD

HIGH
CONCERN
FOR
PERSONHOOD

Congregation

New pastor

LOW CONTROL OF OTHERS
(Submissive behavior)

Figure 4

Biblical Concepts of Leadership

Let me share an observation and then describe some of the insights I have gained in exploring life-giving leadership.

A predominant view among Christians is that effective leaders must be aggressive and act with authority. Many biblical, historical, and current examples could be cited in supporting these traits as fundamental to Christian leadership. But often overlooked are Jesus' teachings related to these traits.

First, Jesus repeatedly stressed that those who lead must adopt a servant, or helping, role. And second, the role of leader is tied not so much to traits or titles as it is to loving others and letting God's Spirit guide.

These teachings at first seemed vague. However, as I struggled to understand them better, I came to the conclusion that Jesus did not intend to tell us *how* to be life-giving leaders; rather his purpose was to tell us what is expected in terms of our growth and the growth of others. Thus, my observation: Christians generally hold a conventional, stereotyped view of leadership while assenting to—though not really comprehending the implications of—Jesus' teachings. Now, in light of this observation, let me relate the three insights.

All Christians are called to be aggressive and to act with authority when appropriate. Christians are not expected to be a submissive people. They are called to transform the world rather than to be changed by it. They must understand and practice their beliefs despite opposition. Whenever Christians must be aggressive and act with authority, their intent must be to fulfill commitments to ministry, mission, and relationship. Their approach may be authoritative but never authoritarian.

All Christians are called to be ministers, or servants, and to submit to the leadership of others when appropriate. Whether serving or submitting to others, a Christian's actions must always be by choice. To do otherwise would be to conform to the expectations of the world, or to be controlled by others. A Christian's actions must be controlled only by his commitment to God and by resulting convictions concerning ministry, mission, and relationship. It is these commitments that free the life-giving leader to be a servant or a follower.

Spiritual gifts represent one key to understanding the Christian approach to leadership. How can we know when to act with authority and when to follow? Teachings related to spiritual gifts indicate that every Christian is given one or more gifts to exercise for the good of others. I have a responsibility to discover, develop, and put into practice that which God has given me.

But I also have a responsibility to help others do the same thing. As I practice my gift I will be assuming responsibility for leadership, and others will follow. And as others use their gifts, I must submit myself to their leadership. It is this give and take, this interdependency, that is the foundation of life-giving leadership and is one way to understanding Jesus' teachings.

Consistent or Inconsistent Leadership

Even with these insights, there was still something about which I was puzzled. It seems, as mentioned above, that the most effective Christian leaders are high in concern for others and are able to assume a high degree of leadership responsibility. They can be assertive and act with authority whenever necessary. Using the action-reaction pattern, Figure 5, it appears that Christian leaders should fall in the circled area.

I accepted this until I realized that not all Christians could be in the circled area. For every leader in the circled area, there must be those within his sphere of influence who tend

HIGH CONTROL OF OTHERS
(Authoritarian behavior)

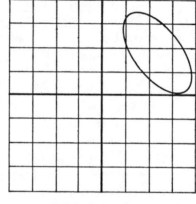

LOW CONCERN FOR PERSONHOOD

HIGH CONCERN FOR PERSONHOOD

LOW CONTROL OF OTHERS
(Submissive behavior)

Figure 5

to be submissive. To produce authoritative Christians a person would have to be essentially a submissive leader.

This conflict was confusing. But the more I examined Jesus' teachings regarding leadership and the biblical passages concerning spiritual gifts, the clearer the concept of life-giving leadership became.

Whereas many leaders develop a consistent pattern of leadership behavior and can be categorized as somewhere between high and low control of others and between high and low concern for personhood, those who are life-giving leaders are inconsistent. Rather, they are consistent in that they are inconsistent: those who lead are also followers, and those who are authoritative are also submissive; yet concern for others is always high.

The (key) to life-giving leadership then is that a leader is sensitive to relationship, can determine the needs of individuals, and can respond accordingly to create opportunities for the growth of all involved. His pattern of action would be more like that illustrated in Figure 6.

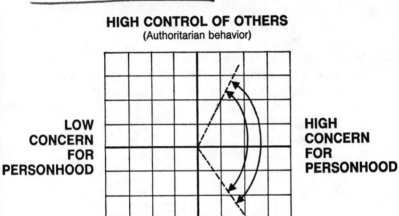

HIGH CONTROL OF OTHERS
(Authoritarian behavior)

LOW CONCERN FOR PERSONHOOD

HIGH CONCERN FOR PERSONHOOD

LOW CONTROL OF OTHERS
(Submissive behavior)

Figure 6

Ideally, this action-reaction pattern would be the same for all Christians as we help and support each other. Rather than being molded by circumstance, we would influence our spiritual development knowing that such efforts are part of God's plan for maturing his people.

With this understanding of life-giving leadership as it relates to others, let's look now at some practical considerations.

Factors That Favor Life-giving Leadership

Life-giving leaders are open to the guidance of God's Spirit. They are aggressive yet very supportive, leading yet serving. Consequently, much of their leadership activity might be categorized as emergent. Being appointed or elected to a position of leadership is an honor but not a necessity for a person to practice life-giving.

In my evaluation of life-giving leadership, people tend to respond most favorably to certain types of behavior and tend to be repelled by other types. Here are some of them:

People like for a leader to be:	*People dislike for a leader to be:*
Friendly	Unfriendly
Truthful	Authoritarian
Hard-working	Manipulative
Open, yet tactful	Lazy
Caring	Tactless
Supportive	Unfeeling
Committed	Laissez-faire
Enthusiastic	Emotionless
Trusting	Suspicious
Group-oriented	Unsure
Emotionally mature	Emotionally immature
Self-confident	Arrogant
Humble	

You could probably add others that have attracted or repulsed you. The important thing to see is that certain types of common, everyday behavior do influence the reactions of others either in a positive or a negative way.

In addition to the basic style of leadership that grows out of the factors listed above, there are several other things that make life-giving leadership successful. More than personality traits or characteristics, these are leadership stances which are freely chosen from a variety of options; they represent the leader's modus operandi.

The life-giving leader seeks to:

- Involve in decision-making those who will be affected.
- Be flexible in meeting changing group needs.
- Distribute leadership responsibilities widely among responsible people rather then centralizing responsibilities among a few.
- Support group values when appropriate and challenge them when necessary.
- Learn from and not be inhibited by the possibility of failure.
- Make decisions based on information and evidence rather than on emotion.
- Maintain a balanced concern for the individual and for the group.
- Encourage the development and use of individual gifts.
- Lead persons to establish and assist them in achieving common goals.
- Maintain a healthy relationship between task and maintenance activities in his own life as well as in organizational life.

Constraints on Life-giving Leadership

Growing out of the foundations of life-giving leadership are four constraints that greatly affect the leadership actions described in subsequent chapters. These constraints may seem to be impositions, but each is freely chosen as a natural expression of life-giving commitments.

Constraint One: That a healthy relationship be sustained between task and maintenance activities

Task activities relate to actions that must be performed in order to accomplish the purpose of an organization. Maintenance activities are those actions taken to sustain a caring, sharing, supportive group environment.

Quite often organizations focus on the tasks that need to be accomplished and expend most of their energy in getting the job done. In such cases when the maintenance or body-building functions are neglected, the cohesiveness among those involved is very shallow, usually limited to the interaction necessary to accomplish the tasks.

An example of this surface cohesion is the congregation that concentrates all its energy on building a new facility. During and immediately following the planning and construction of the building, everything goes well and spirits are high. But often, several months after the dedication, the comment is heard: Things have kind of slacked off; I guess we need to get something else going.

At the other extreme is the organization that stresses mainte-nance, or body building, to the neglect of goal achievement. Such organizations generally have leaders who believe that growing in oneness is the greater value, that task accomplish-ment is a by-product of high morale.

An example of this type of organization is the congregation that expends a majority of its energy over an extended period on searching for who they are and how they relate to God and to each other. They become so absorbed in body building that little attention is given to basic tasks normally expected of a church, such as mission activity.

The life-giving leader understands the relationship between task and maintenance activities and knows that both are impor-tant to the success of an organization. There really is no dichot-omy; ideally, they are mutually supportive, and each makes the other more effective.

The concern of the life-giving leader, however, is focused

not so much on maintaining a balanced emphasis between task and maintenance activities as on maintaining an appropriate relationship. At times a task might take precedence; on another occasion group-building could be the most needed activity. But, regardless, there is always a high degree of concern for getting the job done *and* for doing it in a way that will be growth producing for those involved.

Constraint Two: That a healthy level of tension be maintained

The supposition here is that too much or too little tension is undesirable, and that a certain level is desirable for life-giving purposes.

This constraint comes from the knowledge that learning occurs only in the presence of tension. Without tension there is no reason or motivation for change. But too much tension produces hostility, frustration, and even flight or quitting.

Ideally, enough tension should be present to motivate people to productive action, but not so much that their behavior becomes nonproductive. For the life giver, tension is generally produced by leading people to identify discrepancies between that which they possess and that which they would like to possess in the areas of knowledge, values, and skills. Too much tension is usually the result of overt pressure or manipulation; this is *not* characteristic of life-giving leadership.

A healthy level of tension exists when people are actively identifying and solving the discrepancies in their lives. This is a judgment which the life-giving leader must make: Are people growing, or are they simply existing? The constraint is to maintain sufficient tension to induce personal and corporate growth.

Constraint Three: That a balanced concern be maintained for the individual *and* for the group

The life-giving leader values every person as a unique individual who needs to discover, develop, and put into service gifts provided by God. And it is the leader's responsibility to provide this opportunity.

But while helping individuals, the leader understands that sometimes a concern for individuals can limit or disrupt the growth of a group. Where one person's struggle for growth impedes the growth of others, it is the leader's duty to mediate and to provide the greatest opportunity for all involved.

Constraint Four: That personal growth is necessary if one is to be a life giver

Continual giving demands receiving. No person can remain emotionally and physically healthy unless his own basic needs are met. Thus, there is no conscious effort in life-giving leadership to deny self. It is only as a person honors self that he becomes aware of and can relate effectively to the needs and concerns of others. And it is only as one loves himself that he can truly love and commit himself to a loving God. This concern for God and others, then, is the basis for a continuing renewal of self.

Efforts at self-renewal vary from person to person but generally include individual, small group, and congregational worship; personal development activities such as study, reading, and travel; exploration or soul-searching to know oneself; and associations with persons who encourage self-renewal or help to meet basic relational needs.

One of the characteristics of life-giving leaders is that motivation for personal growth never ceases. Self-development and self-discovery are lifelong endeavors that undergird the process of leading others toward greater maturity in Jesus Christ.

Jesus, the Life Giver

As I have worked with people helping them to understand the principles and implications of life-giving leadership, there is always the wonder that develops as they come to understand what Christian leadership is all about. For these people, Jesus' statement (see John 10:10) that he came that his people might have life and have it abundantly takes on new meaning: that true life comes as Christians see themselves not only as witnesses *to* the Christ but as life givers *with* him. This, then, is the pattern for effective and rewarding Christian leadership. "He who finds his life will lose it, and he who loses [or gives] his life for my sake will find it" (Matt. 10:39, RSV).

3.
Implementing Change

A man bought a horse for sixty dollars and sold it for seventy dollars. Then he bought it back for eighty dollars and later sold it for ninety dollars. How much money did he make in the horse-selling business?

What answer would you give to this fifth-grade math problem? The usual answers are zero, ten, twenty, and thirty dollars.

When introducing the subject of change in leadership seminars, I sometimes use a problem such as this. Each person records an answer without discussion. These are usually fairly well divided among the above answers. Then small groups are asked to discuss the problem, with each person sharing his reasons for selecting a particular answer. After several minutes, each person is asked to record the answer he then believes to be correct.

The results are interesting because most people do not change their answers, and obviously everyone cannot be right. Those who do change their answers report several primary reasons: I wasn't sure, and what someone else said made sense; I'm not so good at math, and several others in my group are smarter; I went along with the group.

Regardless of whether or not people change their answers, there is still a wide variation of responses. And when the correct answer of twenty dollars is announced, there often is laughter and even skepticism because of the simplicity of the calculation. Then we examine the dynamics of our interaction with the problem and with each other.

First, the variety in answers was due to each person analyzing the problem from his own perspective. Based on past experience and whatever expectations may have been present, each person evaluated the problem and stated what he believed to be the correct response. In recording an answer, each person was making a commitment, however slight.

Second, most people do not change because to do so they must doubt the accuracy of their answers and be willing to admit they are wrong. And with what appears to be a simple problem, there is little reason to doubt one's answer or to risk one's ego.

The third point is that when a person tries to convince another to change his answer, the response is usually negative. Such attempts convey the impression that the sender of the message believes he is correct and the other person is wrong. Under such circumstances two-way communication is very limited; people are talking *at* rather than *with* one another.

What Is Change?

In its most basic form, change is simply the development or alteration of something. In terms of human behavior, change is related to modifications in three general areas: cognitive (related to knowledge), affective (related to emotions), and psychomotor (related to physical skills).

Changes in these three areas do not just happen. They are elicited as a person responds to various stimuli in his life. These stimuli may be natural such as the growth-producing hormones in a child's body, or they may be planned such as the learning activities provided by a teacher.

Change is complex in that modifications in one area affect and are affected by the other areas. So, in examining change, keep in mind that any breakdown into areas in which change occurs is just to understand and to project the direction of change.

Why Study Change?

The life-giving leader is in the business of initiating change. He is continually seeking to elicit in others the commitments and actions that lead toward Christian maturity and ministry. This is not unique, for, as indicated earlier, every person by action or inaction does cause changes in others. But for the life-giving leader, the response of others is not taken for granted nor is the direction of change considered random. Rather the *direction* of change must be based on values inherent in the Christian faith and the *process* to achieve change based on the principles of life-giving leadership.

Planned change, those intentional actions to assist people in developing or modifying something, is treated here with a desire that it be used for life-giving purposes. The strategies and techniques suggested are consistent with the Christian faith, but it must be pointed out that they are not good in themselves. It is the leader's knowledge of and ability to use them that determines their value. Thus a skilled leader can use this process to achieve life-giving aims.

The alternative to understanding change is to be subject to a variety of internal and external forces that may or may not support your values and/or goals. This often results in living or in leading in a random manner which tends to convey a confusion of values or a lack of skill. Consequently, one's leadership ability is impaired. Change strategy used without understanding can actually confuse and thwart desired change.

These reasons for studying the change process are based on the assumptions that planned change is viable for achieving Christian growth and that a leader who has an understanding of and skills in implementing change will be more effective than one who does not. This implies that the content and process involved in implementing change will be consistent with, not contrary to, the basic principles of life-giving leadership.

Life-giving Leadership and Change

The basic commitments of life-giving leadership are opposed to the use of power as a change strategy. Whereas changes might be implemented more efficiently, there is little regard for the effect on and feelings of those involved.

Experts may know what is best, but to place total reliance on them not only fosters dependence but also avoids the biblical injunction that every Christian possesses and is to use his talents (gifts) for the good of others (see 1 Pet. 4:10). The use of experts in pursuing change then is not necessarily the most desirable method; but the concept need not be contrary to life-giving commitments. The manner in which expertise is used would determine the viability of this approach for Christians.

The discrepancy approach to change is most consistent with life-giving principles. Through a process of evaluation and projection, individuals determine for themselves those changes which are desirable and to which they will commit themselves.

How Leaders Produce Change

Power

There are basically three ways in which changes occur. The first is in response to power. Whenever we are made to do something or perceive that we must do something, we are changing or acting because of the influence of a greater power (whether or not we agree with that power).

Expertise

The second approach to change is that which is elicited in response to acknowledged or perceived expertise. This differs from the previous approach because there is no power to compel change. Changes that occur are due to the belief that an authority has spoken, therefore compliance should follow.

Discrepancy

This approach is dependent on an awareness of a discrepancy between that which exists and that which is desired. Change may be motivated by external influences, but the decision to respond is based on an inner desire to achieve some benefit not currently possessed.

This differs from other approaches in that persons are involved in evaluating that which exists and in projecting the potential of changes. The role of leadership also differs. Rather than seeking to enforce change or to convince people that leaders know what is best, the intent is to educate people and provide assistance as they explore and pursue ways to achieve that which they deem of value.

The chart on page 39 provides a graphic description of the assumptions and expectations underlying the three approaches to change.

Approaches to Change

	Power	Expertise	Discrepancy
Basic Assumption of Leaders	Leaders know what is best	Experts know what is best	People when properly informed can make intelligent decisions
Role of Leaders	Make and enforce decisions	Be or rely on experts	Provide education; involve people in decision-making
Basic Assumption of People	Comply or face the consequences	Experts know what is best therefore people should follow their advice	With appropriate information people can assume responsibility for decisions affecting their lives
Role of People	Compliance	Acceptance	Involvement

This approach recognizes the value of every person and his right to be involved in making decisions and in working to achieve changes that will affect his life.

Whereas experts may be consulted or an authoritative stance may be necessitated, the general change strategy is to assist people in reflecting on and evaluating that which exists and projecting that which is needed. The difference between that which exists and that which is needed is the discrepancy. And when this is identified by a person for himself, the foundation for change—and the motivation to achieve that change—is laid.

This does not imply that change automatically follows or that it will be easy. Such is just the first step in a change strategy that is dependent on voluntary participation and is insistent on the growth of all involved.

Basic Criterion for Change

Random change is neither desirable nor emotionally healthy for most people. So to cause a person to want to change there must be a reason that will answer the questions: What is in it for me? What benefit will be provided? Or, relating this to the discrepancy approach, "Is the benefit something that will alleviate the discrepancy which has been identified?"

Let me be more practical with a personal example. I enjoy relaxing after work in our reclining, easy chair. With a glass of iced tea within reach, I just settle back, read the newspaper, and soak up the good, relaxed feeling.

One evening, while engrossed in the paper, I heard our young son scream. Immediately my restful state was disturbed, and I faced a problem—there was a discrepancy between what had existed and the reality of the moment. In other words, I was moved from a safe and secure condition into an unsure or unsteady state of being. And one thing a human being cannot tolerate is an unsteady, tension-producing condition.

There are basically two responses to tension: seek to alleviate it by either solving the problem or by escaping from it. Thinking back later, I couldn't ignore the scream so I automatically used the problem-solving process. I remember evaluating in a moment the intensity and quality of the yell, the direction from which it came, those with whom he was playing, the location of my wife, and the play equipment in the yard. I could have made any number of responses in an attempt to solve the problem, but I had to pick the response that would be best for me based on my assessment of the situation.

Often a scream from our son is solved by ignoring it or by calling out, "What's the matter?" But in this case, the quality of his voice indicated that he was in real pain and not just angry or slightly wounded (as often happened). Well, my solution was to rush to his aid and then proceed to clean and doctor a stubbed toe.

Later I went back to the easy chair and gradually returned to a steady, relaxed state, the problem having been solved.

This, in a capsule, is how change works—awareness of and efforts to solve problems so that tension is kept at a minimum. Now, obviously, the solution of one problem does not indicate a new pattern of behavior. But it does provide information that will affect subsequent actions. The point is that a change agent must understand and use these natural principles that are always operating. Rather than contriving ways of leading people to change, he should build on the innate need of man to solve his problems.

Problem-Solving as a Strategy

The basic approach to change, then, is problem-solving. Whether used instinctively or as a scientific methodology, by novice or by scientist, it is the natural process for finding answers. The procedure is: (1) What is the problem? (2) What are some alternatives for solving it? (3) Which alternative will most likely solve the problem? (4) Testing of proposed solution, and (5) If the problem is not solved satisfactorily, repeat the process using the information gained.

The difference between the novice and the professional is that the professional has a greater degree of expertise in understanding and managing the various factors involved and resources available. But the novice uses the same process and, based on his perception, knowledge and ability, solves problems the best way he can.

Here, again, the role of life-giving leadership is to use the normal problem-solving process but with the skill of a professional as he works to achieve desirable change. This involves assisting people in

- Identifying and evaluating problems
- Finding possibilities for solving problems
- Evaluating possibilities and potential results if proposed solutions are implemented
- Implementing the most appropriate solutions
- Learning from attempts at problem solving so that future attempts will utilize information gained from previous experiences.

Role of Discontent

Discontent is important to life-giving leaders for two reasons. As illustrated earlier, an unsteady state of being is the prelude to some type of action; and it is discontent that often creates such a situation. When discontent develops in a situation for which the leader is responsible, he must assist people in dealing with the problem in a positive, healthy life-giving way.

The other reason relates primarily to change that is planned or initiated by the leader. If there is no discontent, there is no motivation for change. Hence, the leader must be in the position of eliciting discontent that will lead to a consideration of proposed change.

This must be done so that the tension produced will motivate those involved to identify and solve the problem causing the tension. The role of the leader is not to create problems indiscriminately but to create situations in which persons can identify discrepancies between where they are and where they would like to be in terms of knowledge, attitudes, or skills—thus the self-identified discrepancy.

A Strategy for Implementing Change

Rather than begin this chapter with a strategy for implementing planned change, I chose to describe the principles related to change; this was done to assist you in understanding why and how the various steps in the following strategy are interrelated.

Here, again, the process is not uniquely Christian; the same strategy can be used for constructive or for manipulative purposes. It is, however, the most effective approach to change for life-giving leadership. And when so used, it will assist people in growing and maturing as well as in accomplishing changes they deem desirable.

This diagram is a rather simplistic representation of a complex process. The arrows indicate sequential actions, but this is only theoretical; rarely are such idealistic situations encountered. Keep in mind that at any time—due to a change in

Change?

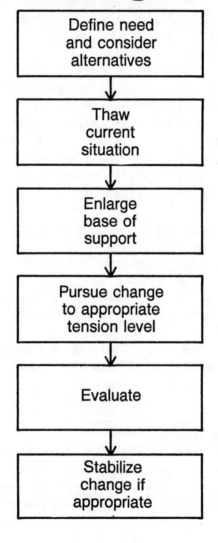

Define need
and consider
alternatives

↓

Thaw
current
situation

↓

Enlarge
base of
support

↓

Pursue change
to appropriate
tension level

↓

Evaluate

↓

Stabilize
change if
appropriate

the environment, new information, and such—it may be necessary to revert to a previous stage or to the beginning. But for understanding, I will proceed systematically through the process.

Stage One: Define Need/Consider Alternatives

The first stage parallels the initial steps in the problem-solving process. It is imperative to evaluate the need and define in detail the problem(s). This must be done accurately, taking into account not only the empirical data (the facts) but also the feelings and perceptions of persons involved. While feelings and perceptions are not generally considered part of the scientific approach to problem-solving, they do exert significant influence on change efforts in which high value is placed on personhood.

After completing a precise analysis of the need, alternatives for solving the problem must be gathered. Some alternatives will emerge from the past experiences of those involved; others must be gleaned from a variety of sources such as knowledgeable persons and reference materials.

At times there will be no clear alternatives that promise a solution. In such cases, fresh thinking and creativity are necessary to assemble potential solutions.

From the variety of alternatives, those that seem to be viable must be selected and then ranked according to potential for solving the problem effectively and efficiently. This ranking procedure involves two indispensable assessments—analysis of the forces involved and calculation of the cost-benefit factor.

Force-field Analysis.—Made popular by Kurt Lewin, this assessment is made to determine the forces supporting a particular change and the forces resisting that change. The idea is that there is a force field surrounding the introduction of any change. Forces may be of any type, such as environmental, educational, cultural, organizational, personal, or economic. They may be direct or indirect, combined or isolated in exerting influence. But the basic premise is that the status quo exists at the point where these forces are balanced, as illustrated on page 47.

Accordingly, the only ways to implement change are (1) to increase the forces favoring change; (2) to decrease the forces resisting change; or (3) to cause a redirection of the forces opposing change so that they either come to support or, at least, do not interfere with the proposed change.

The simplest way to perform a force-field analysis is to sketch a diagram similar to that on page 47. Place in the middle the potential change. List all of the supporting forces on the left side and all the opposing forces on the right. Include individual and organized forces, even those that seem remote. Next to each force listed, indicate with some code the probable strength of that force (for example, low, medium, or high).

Now compare the opposed forces and their strengths. Refer to the three ways in which change may be achieved. What must be done in order to pursue implementation of the proposed change?

Here are some guidelines. Avoid simply strengthening the support for change; this is an appeal to power. Opposition can be overcome in this way but the personhood of those standing in the way is often violated, thereby making the process counterproductive.

Eliminating resisting forces may be more subtle than strengthening support but may be perceived as manipulation and thus should be approached with caution. A good rule to follow is that if people are directly related to any of the forces that you would seek to add or delete, avoid doing either. Use

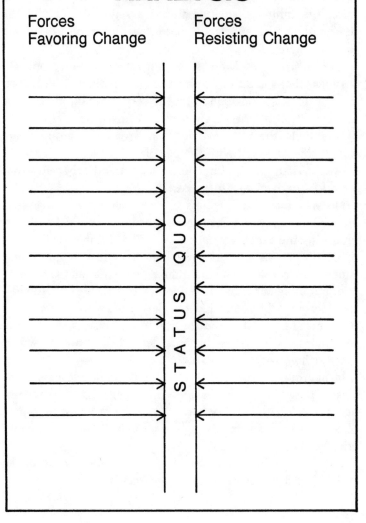

FORCE-FIELD ANALYSIS

Forces
Favoring Change

Forces
Resisting Change

STATUS QUO

these two approaches primarily when dealing with things, not with persons.

The third approach, seeking to redirect forces which may oppose or inhibit change, is always a viable strategy for the life-giving leader and is the basis for the process described in this chapter.

· *Cost-benefit Factor.*—The cost-benefit factor is the second assessment that should be made before proceeding with planned change. This is a calculation that is very common in business and industry but not widely used in Christian circles.

Essentially, the costs involved in making a change are determined and compared with the benefits that the change would provide. Then the question is raised: Are the benefits that would be derived worth the cost?

No well-managed business concern plans for change—no matter how attractive the potential benefits—until the cost of producing the benefits is determined. The cost may be in terms of tangible items such as equipment, facilities, supplies, and contracts. Or it may be more intangible such as employee morale, public relations, and competitor response. Nevertheless, all costs must be calculated for they are a part of the price that must be paid to produce the desired results. And, as is sometimes the case, the benefits desired may not be worth the cost involved.

In figuring the cost-benefit factor, life-giving leaders must be sure to review the forces opposing change that were identified in the force-field analysis. Often these forces will be part of the cost of pursuing change, especially if they are people oriented.

To calculate the cost-benefit factor, divide a sheet of paper with a line down the middle as illustrated.

COST-BENEFIT FACTOR

Potential Costs: Potential Benefits:

1. _____   1. _____
2. _____   2. _____
3. _____   3. _____
4. _____   4. _____
5. _____   5. _____
6. _____   6. _____
7. _____   7. _____

Review all of the proposed benefits and list those that might realistically be achieved. Then determine the costs as accurately as possible and list them on the opposite side of the sheet.

For benefits or costs of an objective nature (for example materials, labor, equipment, facilities), secure or provide reliable estimates of the value that will be added and/or the costs that will be incurred. List these first in the appropriate column.

Subjective benefits and costs (for example morale, commitment, and attitudes of people both inside and outside the organization) are more difficult to predict. Nevertheless some type of judgment must be made. Try to include not only the immediate effect but an approximation of long-range results.

Now review the total package of benefits and costs. Is there a difference between the benefits that are desired and those actually anticipated. Are the benefits and costs which are listed realistic? What is the relationship between the benefits that are anticipated and the costs that will be incurred? (This relationship is the cost-benefit factor.)

A Calculation.—Some changes may not be worth the cost involved or may not be viable at a particular time; so it is at this point in the process that a go or no-go decision should be made.

With the information available from the force-field analysis and from the cost-benefit factor, persons involved will have to make a decision. Among leaders in business and industry, the decision is based on the promise of a return greater than the investment—and this is usually expressed in dollars.

Among life-giving leaders, however, there are many times when the cost in terms of time, energy, and emotional strain—as well as money—might far exceed any tangible benefits. Yet a decision will be made to attempt change simply because of the Christian commitments involved.

The calculation, then, must of necessity be partially subjective. In making a decision, remember that any change is possible given enough time, energy, and other resources (which are part of the cost). And for Christians, any attempt at change should be based on life-giving principles.

Stage Two: Thaw Current Situation

As pointed out earlier in this chapter, without some dissatisfaction with the current situation there is no potential or motivation for change. (Remember that this strategy is based on the self-identified discrepancy approach to change. Thus the attitudes and commitments of those who will be affected must be considered.) So in this stage, motivation for planned change must be initiated. This basically involves enabling people to determine for themselves that there are some worthwhile goals that they would like to achieve and that there is a discrepancy between these goals and the status quo.

In order to thaw the current situation, people must be led

to envision or see demonstrated on a small scale that which is proposed. This is what is usually referred to as the vision-model approach.

The vision is what people create in their minds in response to a stimulus or situation. Involved in forming the vision are all of the pros and cons of potential change with the most important consideration being: Why should I (we)? For a vision to be effective in thawing rather than reinforcing the current situation, people must be able to identify benefits which they would like to attain.

Whenever people perceive that these potential benefits are lacking in the current situation, there is potential for discontent. And the stronger people desire the potential benefits, the greater the discontent and thus potential for change.

A model is an example or a small-scale creation incorporating the potential changes so that people can observe the benefits firsthand. Rather than having to create visions, there is something concrete from which dreams can evolve and discrepancies emerge.

Ideally, leadership will use visioning and modeling in complementing roles. But each does have specialized uses. For example, visioning—being essentially a mental activity—can be done rather quickly and easily but is dependent on people's willingness to explore new possibilities. Modeling, however, is dependent on developing and/or using a physical representation that conveys the desired benefits; and this is sometimes difficult or time-consuming, especially when benefits are not readily apparent. But modeling is sometimes the only way to begin if people are not willing to explore possibilities for change.

A church's educational program can make an important contribution to the thawing process as people are exposed to new ideas and ways of doing things. Through regularly scheduled, low-threat learning experiences, leaders can create awareness, understanding, and even motivation concerning potential change.

Whereas education will certainly be used later to implement change, at this stage its purpose is to gain exposure in order to create within individuals a self-identified discrepancy.

Stage Three: Enlarge Base of Support

As indicated in the force-field analysis, a necessary part of eliciting change is redirecting the forces that oppose change so that they either support or at least do not resist the proposed change. These forces may be redirected by giving attention to several basic principles.

1. *Strengthen relationships.*—Good interpersonal relationships increase the level of trust and open channels of communication. As mutual trust increases and as people openly discuss the discrepancies they feel, esprit de corps develops. This enables people to explore together new ideas and ways of doing things that would not normally be attempted individually.

2. *Pursue discussion.*—Don't underestimate the value of open and free discussion—both formal and informal—concerning anticipated changes. Information regarding proposed changes and potential effects can do much to allay the resistance often displayed when people face something that is unknown. Unless people understand what is taking place, they become threatened and seek to preserve things as they are. Discussion also allows people to express their feelings, to hear the opinions of others faced with the same changes, and to explore the potential advantages and disadvantages of the proposed changes—all necessary ingredients in implementing change.

3. *Seek consensus.*—Through open discussion in an environment of mutual trust, Christians can work toward consensus. The more people whose ideas and concerns are reflected in proposed changes, the easier change will proceed. Majority rule, as practiced in many church business sessions, disregards the principle that the church is not a true democratic organization; it is a theodemocracy. That is, democratic procedures are followed, but the goal always is to determine God's leadership. And this is best understood as Christians work toward consensus—through discussion, study, prayer, and constant reflection on the meaning of any decisions that will be made.

Seeking consensus, then, may involve a modification of the timing, degree, and/or character of proposed change. As more people become involved, there must be give and take so that the proposed change becomes generally acceptable. This does not mean that the basic *intent* of the change is negotiable, for it is based on a specific need defined before considering change. But the manner in which the need is to be met is negotiable. And it is in this give and take that creative energies can be focused on a solution to the problem, all the while increasing the size of the constituency that supports the proposed change.

Basically stated, change is accomplished most readily when people who will be affected are involved in the decision-making process.

4. *Stress benefits.*—Do not try to sell people on change; help them to envision the advantages that might be gained from change. Salesmen refer to this as selling the sizzle instead of the steak.

For example, an insurance representative never tries to sell an insurance policy. Rather he offers a means for saving periodically, financial protection for your family, and a college education for children. A car salesman uses a different approach; he sells style, safety, economy, prestige, carefree maintenance, and comfort.

The idea is to determine the need or discrepancy that will be met by the change you have to "sell." Each need that will be met is a benefit to emphasize whenever discussing the merits of proposed change. If benefits are varied, accentuate those most pertinent for the occasion and/or the people involved. The response will be in direct proportion to the degree that people feel the needs and perceive that the proposed change will meet those needs.

5. *Work with the legitimizers.*—Every group has persons who can expedite or hinder the change process. These are people from whom others take their cue—knowingly or unknowingly. Extra time spent in relating to these people as suggested above may provide great benefits in terms of expediting change. Two cautions, however: act with integrity, and don't seek to enlist a legitimizer to bring about change through his own personal charisma. Reaching the legitimizers must be just one more means of enlarging the base of support for planned change.

Stage Four: Pursue Change to Appropriate Tension Level

As appropriate changes are implemented, it is necessary to monitor the degree of change and the pace of change. The ideal is to move rapidly enough to produce creative, problem-solving tension but not so fast as to produce a fight-or-flight response.

Keep tuned in to people's feelings and watch for signs of frustration. What good things are happening? What unhealthy signs do you detect? Here are some of the more common signs to look for in monitoring the change process. Think of them as being on a continuum from healthy to unhealthy.

Indications of Healthy Tension Level	*Indications of Unhealthy Tension Level*
Steady/increased participation	Decreasing participation
Discussing opportunities	Discussing reasons why not
Expressing feelings of excitement	Feelings of pessimism
Looking forward to meetings	No expectancy
Actively dealing with issues	Avoiding issues; emotional rabbit chasing
Focused on purpose	Focused on past
Caring environment	Factions/infighting
Open, trusting communication	Calculated, guarded communication

Each of these signals is not an absolute indication; but taken together, a pattern begins to develop. This enables leaders to analyze the situation as change progresses. As actions of persons involved indicate a tendency toward a healthy tension level, the degree and pace of change can continue and/or increase. However, as actions indicate a tendency toward an unhealthy tension level, the degree and pace must be lessened. The key is to adjust as necessary based on a continued assessment of the situation.

Lest we overlook one point, there is another remote yet possible response by those involved: apathy or disinterest. If things continue just as they have been, if people do not even react, the planning for change has missed its mark. This is what might be called a laissez-faire response; that is, there is little or no emotional attachment to the change—either pro or con—so people can take it or leave it.

In this case, the larger body just may not feel or appreciate the need for change. If this happens, there is little choice but to revert to an earlier stage of the change process; then use the experience and information gained to evaluate and project new directions.

Stage Five: Evaluate

Informal evaluation is a natural part of all stages of planned change. During this stage, however, a systematic, thorough evaluation should be initiated. Leaders must determine what is happening in relation to accomplishing the desired change and in the response of persons involved.

At this point in the process, repeat the force-field analysis and reassess the cost-benefit factor. Determine the extent to which desired benefits have been achieved. Evaluate the content of the change and the process through which change has been pursued.

What is the immediate effect? This is perhaps the strongest influence on reaction to change. But the life-giving leader must look beyond that which is apparent and assist people in projecting and evaluating long-range effects. We must not only consider change that is beneficial for us, but we must be aware of the way our decisions may affect others—present and future.

Consider the situation of a midtown congregation that ten years ago obligated itself heavily over a twenty-year period to start a Christian day school. Today the make-up of that congregation has changed and a majority feel that too much of their church budget goes to support a school which many children in the congregation do not attend. Why, these people say, must mission gifts and church program needs suffer in order to support a school so desired a decade ago but a millstone around our necks today? Could this situation have been averted? Possibly, by some astute leaders who could have helped people see beyond themselves to potential consequences of their actions on others.

Through an analysis of the present situation and future implications, reflection on the consequences of similar changes pursued by others, and prayerful searching for God's leadership, persons involved can come to a decision concerning the appropriateness of changes which have evolved. Undesirable change should be abandoned or corrective efforts initiated by returning to any appropriate stage in the change process.

Desirable change that is to be a part of the ongoing lifestyle of a congregation is ready for stabilization and reinforcement.

Stage Six: Stabilize Appropriate Change

For planned change to be lasting, it is imperative that changes become an accepted part of some ongoing system. That is, whatever has changed must not continuously be supported by outside forces or be perceived by those affected as an imposition.

It is the role of leaders therefore to sever gradually the dependency relationship that has been established. Through judicious use of reinforcement and training and gradual withdrawal from involvement in decision-making, leaders can assist followers in assuming responsibility for and deriving benefits from changes introduced. In effect, stabilization of change requires a withdrawal of the support system that has birthed the new life. That which is left is a part of the ongoing system, perhaps not even belonging to those who may have first envisioned it. The greatest compliment for the life-giving introducer of change comes after the dependency relationship is severed, when the people say, "Look what we did."

In order to stabilize change, leaders must assist in reinforcing whatever is desirable about the change. Newly acquired attitudes, knowledge, skills, and such must be used successfully; satisfaction must be experienced, appropriate recognition received, and desired benefits achieved. If the change has developed through the stages described and leaders have followed life-giving principles, it is easy to reinforce change since that which has developed has been a natural outgrowth rather than something imposed.

Leaders can assist by giving encouragement, providing appropriate recognition, assisting with continuing development, maintaining open communication, and assisting persons in experiencing success in dealing with the change.

In addition to reinforcement, the other major contributor to stabilization is the increasing involvement of people in the decision-making process. As in the following illustration, persons should gradually be led to a point of accepting major responsibility for decision-making related to changes in which they are involved.

It is the role of the leader, without abdicating any responsibility, to move gradually from a stance of authoritative guid-

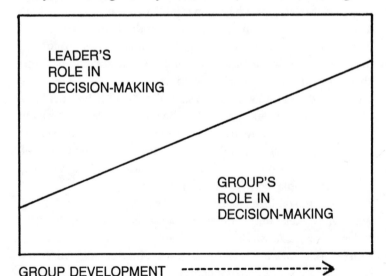

LEADER'S
ROLE IN
DECISION-MAKING

GROUP'S
ROLE IN
DECISION-MAKING

GROUP DEVELOPMENT -------------------->

ance to a position of encourager and enabler; this is necessary so that others can make and accept responsiblity for decisions related to their lives.

The Environment for Change

Continual change is harmful to one's health as was illustrated popularly by Alvin Toffler in *Future Shock* and in a more scholarly manner by Paul Tournier in *A Place for You*. Both of these authors cite the emotional and physical stress that develops when people experience an overload on their adaptive system.

But the type of change that normally produces unhealthy stress is imposed change, not change that results from the efforts of persons to meet discrepancies which they have identified in their lives. Therefore, an environment that encourages continuing evaluation and adjustment must be founded on the principle that planned change (such as presented in this chapter) must be for and ultimately by the people affected.

One caution: there is always a danger of counterproductive actions in pursuing change. No matter how committed the leadership or congregation, there are chances for error; and often these will not be apparent until a mistake has been made. Most errors, fortunately, can be corrected or forgiven, and the change process can proceed to a rewarding end. But there is no excuse for one very common error: using a process, or means, that is not consistent with the result desired.

Christians must always be aware of the desired end—that persons be led toward full expression of the life and teachings of Jesus Christ. Shortcuts to this end means that are not consonant with this high calling, have no place in life-giving leadership.

All means, obviously, cannot be categorized, therefore leaders will need to evaluate their methods and their motives. But this in itself is a part of life-giving leadership, always reflecting, evaluating, and projecting in the light of basic Christian principles. Planned change must not be viewed as an end; rather it should be seen as a means in achieving maximum expression and fulfillment in the Christian life and mission.

4.
Working with People in Groups—I

Life-giving leadership does not function in isolation; it is with, for, and through people. Thus, one's effectiveness as a leader can be measured to a great extent by his ability to elicit, combine, and focus the energy of people on achieving common goals. Hence, the purpose of this chapter—to describe the content and methodology of a life-giving approach to group leadership.

Group and Leadership Roles

Much of the Christian life is pursued in community. This is the biblical expectation—that we function as a body, to fulfill commitments to mission and ministry. Groups may be large or small, structured or unstructured, but all have as a focus some aspect of support and development related to the church and/or to group members. The role of groups, therefore, is to provide a means through which participants can channel their efforts to meet common concerns that could not effectively be met through individual action.

It is the role of group leadership to assist people in (1) clarifying the reason for existence, (2) formulating guidelines for fulfilling this reason or purpose, and (3) interacting in accord with group expectations.

A life-giving leader is not a director; he is a facilitator of human interaction based on personal commitments regarding mission, ministry, and relationship. Consequently, the emphasis in this chapter is on the development and interaction of all group members and resources. This is in direct contrast to a leader-centered approach wherein control and direction are determined primarily by the leader (whether or not this style is accepted or desired by group members). A life-giving leader gives himself to the group and functions as an enabler, with all the convictions, understandings, and integrity described in earlier chapters.

Bringing People Together

The basic responsibility of leadership is to bring people together. This involves not only physical presence but common will and spirit. Generally, people have varied expectations and appear quite unsure about why they are together or how they are to proceed. But through understanding leadership, expectations can be merged and cohesiveness developed in such a way that the group can satisfactorily achieve its purpose.

How does this happen? There are identifiable growth stages through which all groups progress. As a leader understands and becomes more proficient in guiding groups through various stages, meetings become more productive and people experience more pleasure in being together.

The pattern for group development moves through five stages. Each stage is a prerequisite for the subsequent stages, and the process can always revert to the first stage. Once a group has moved through all stages, however, it may revert to an earlier stage; but it can return much more easily to the last and most desirable operating level.

1. Dependence—("THIS IS JOHN SMITH'S GROUP.")

This is the get-acquainted and small-talk stage of group life. Actions basically are initiated by and communication flows through the leader. Group members look to the leader to initiate actions.

Comments that might be heard include: "Tell us how you want this done. Why are we together? You're the leader!" When identifying the group, members will often refer to it by using the leader's name, "I'm in John Smith's group." Basically, group members feel little commitment to each other or to the group during this stage. They are dependent on John Smith, and all leadership responsibility is his.

Many groups never develop beyond this stage, consequently individual growth and group cohesiveness are not realized. Usually, this occurs with a short-term, highly task-oriented group that meets simply to get its job done. Or, sometimes a leader who is unaware of or unwilling to risk the potential benefits of moving to the next stage maintains control and *directs* the group. This is not in accord with life-giving principles.

People who are brought together and operate only at this stage of group development focus primarily on the task to be performed. There is little personal and group growth as might be expressed through a caring, sharing, and supportive fellowship.

2. Counter-Independence—("YOU'RE THE LEADER!")

For the life-giving leader, moving the group to the second stage—counter-independence—is a prerequisite to growth for all involved. To provide opportunity for members to move to this stage, the leader begins to loose his hold on the group—providing freedom to explore, develop, and create within whatever guidelines that may exist. Members often resist these efforts due to a slight amount of tension that develops.

A leader may suggest a sharing of expectations related to the group or an open discussion concerning how members would like to handle meetings. Or an assignment may be given such as, "Choose two or three other people and write down five things you would like to study during the next three months." The result is often met with resistance expressed politely as, "Would you give us more information?" or "Tell us exactly what you have in mind." In other instances, the comments may be rather pointed, such as, "You're the leader; just tell us."

This stage produces an uneasy feeling and sometimes even a hostile environment perceived both by the leader and by participants. This is normal, however, and need not frighten anyone. Leaders, unaware, sometimes stumble into this stage and become uneasy as the tension develops; they then rush to take charge and revert to the dependency stage.

An example of this is a Sunday School teacher who described to me her desire to involve her class in group discussion and other participation-type learning activities. However, she always ended up lecturing. After discussing the stages of group development, she decided that whenever she looked to the class for participation and response, she felt uncomfortable because she was not in control and members didn't always respond; this caused her always to revert to lecturing—a very controlling yet secure type of leadership.

The key to this stage is to involve members in the life and purpose of the group. Expectations are discussed, members begin to interact, and the leader gradually steps out of an authority role.

3. **Counter-Dependence**—("THE LEADER IS NOT ONE OF US.")

As the previous stage gives way to counter-dependence, group members begin flexing their collective muscles. They begin enjoying each other and actively seek to influence the life of the group. They discover that they do not have to be dependent on the leader (or some authority figure or structure) and openly resist at opportune times. This sometimes is characterized as an adolescent rebellion: "We don't have to do it his way (or the way it has always been done)."

Members begin to think for themselves, speak openly, and direct conversation to each other rather than to the leader. Chatter is frequent, and often what the leader has to offer is lost in the interaction among members.

The danger here is that the leader will not understand this seemingly nonproductive behavior. To those who do not understand, this stage appears wasted time. How often I have heard a leader shout for attention or clap hands, then proceed to reestablish control over the group and revert to the dependency stage, thereby squashing hopes for growth to group maturity.

During this stage, the leader simply has to endure and love—supporting but not controlling, guiding but not parenting group members. The adolescent group is reaching for maturity.

4. **Independence**—("WE CAN DO IT BY OURSELVES.")

If the group is allowed to develop, a point will come when members find themselves operating apart from the influence of the leader. There will be a time or times when members speak directly to each other, make decisions, and interact oblivious to the leader. Then the group members may inform the leader what has been decided or how something will be done. The group may even choose to meet without the leader.

This stage is the most difficult for the leader to endure for the feeling is one of loss of control and even failure. The leader may perceive that his leadership is rejected or that he is not needed. Some leaders, not understanding, are hurt (and react accordingly) or venture to take control in a struggle for power. Either action produces a no-win situation.

A life-giving leader endures the group's struggle for independence and provides support, guidance, and encouragement as appropriate. He does not seek to master or regain control, for to do so would thwart the next growth step so eagerly awaited.

5. Interdependence—("THIS IS OUR GROUP.")

As group members perceive that the leader is caring, supportive, and not controlling, the threat diminishes and the leader becomes accepted as a member of the group and as leader. He is seen as a resource person and co-worker rather than as an authority figure. Leadership becomes more a function to be shared by all group members rather than invested in one person.

Cohesiveness and spirit are high in this stage, enabling the group to operate at maximum effectiveness. In addition to shared leadership, characteristics may include extensive participation and decision-making by members, open discussion of ideas, sharing of concerns, increased expressions of commitment to the group, a high level of trust among participants, and an increasing willingness to venture forth into new, even high-risk, situations.

John Smith, group leader and director, has become group enabler, helper, and guide. The biggest compliment that can be paid is for members to proclaim, "Look what *we* did."

This is bringing people together. It is enabling them to become more than a collection of individuals; they become a body that in many ways has power beyond itself. In interdependence, they have the freedom to be dependent as need arises, to build on the gifts of various members, to challenge, to struggle, to share, and to achieve. An interdependent group is a life-giving group, and God in his own way can elicit a response and growth that can empower such a body to contribute their part in Christian mission and ministry.

Some Observations

Progression through stages may be rapid or slow. Group development is predictable, but timing related to the various stages is imprecise due to the variety of backgrounds and interpersonal styles among members. Whereas one group may pass through all stages in a few hours, another group will take weeks or months of interaction. And, then, some groups never progress beyond a particular stage. Leadership ability and experience of group members are the major determining factors.

Another influence on timing is the expectation each member holds related to group interaction. Persons who have experienced and value interdependence move easily toward this stage; others who have experienced primarily dependency or the tension associated with some of the intermediate stages are more resistant. The leader must be sensitive to all members and seek to elicit understanding and development at an appropriate rate.

As necessary, this involves relating to persons individually and/or tailoring group experiences to meet a variety of expectations and needs. Since group development involves change for many people, many of the change principles presented earlier apply.

Life-giving leadership will naturally encourage movement through the various stages; the influence of the leader will generally be greater at the beginning and gradually decrease as the group begins to mature.

This progression does *not* degrade the role of the leader; it only signifies a conscious adjustment from director to enabler, from one who supervises to one who serves.

As shown earlier in the action-reaction pattern description, this progression isn't necessarily direct; rather it is situational and changes based on the needs of those involved. The direction, however, is always toward full expression of the gifts and calling of members individually and as a body.

The leader faces tension. Tension can be endured if you understand it and recognize that it is a normal part of the maturing process. As groups move into the counterdependence and independence stages, a sensitive leader often feels hurt; but any move toward personally resolving the tension-producing situation will prove counterproductive. The group must move through the stages, with the leader guiding rather than controlling.

Knowing that tension will come is helpful but makes no less real those harsh expressions aimed at the leader. It is uncomfortable but not unbearable. Tension is simply part of the growth process.

Reflection provides an opportunity for learning. Looking back, members can discuss feelings and share evaluations related to their growth as a group. They can explore the relationships and struggles for influence that were a part of the growth process. Such an evaluation can be done periodically in an informal way.

Even after the group has the ability to function interdependently, occasional process evaluations will strengthen and maintain the cohesiveness of the group as well as improve functions which are task related. Leadership responsibility includes calling for reflection and evaluation whenever appropriate.

Appearances may be deceiving. A life-giving leader may appear to be subordinating his own desires and commitments to the will of the group. But as pointed out earlier, every action is by choice. Rather than being committed to organizing people in support of a personal cause, the leader focuses on enabling people to identify and pursue causes to which *they* are committed.

So long as group purposes are in accord with the principles of life-giving leadership, the leader supports and encourages. Whenever discrepancies arise, the life-giving leader calls for evaluation in light of commitments related to mission, ministry, and relationship.

As illustrated with the action-reaction pattern, the leader adjusts as the situation demands, always seeking to provide the opportunity for personal and corporate growth.

There will always be no-grows. Invariably you will be involved with some people who simply do not value growth—for themselves or for others. They will be the ones who always encourage dependence on the leader; they react negatively to any persons who begin to risk in search of growth.

Fortunately, these people are usually in the minority and serve only as a minor deterrent to group development. Sometimes, however, these persons gravitate to the same group; they want a director-leader who will not disturb them but will run the show. The life-giving leader generally experiences frustration when working with such a group over an extended period.

Do not expend an inordinate amount of energy trying to lead people to grow. Jesus taught us to accept reality—that some people will not respond—and move on to encourage and influence others. Life-giving leaders must accept the fact that they cannot be all things to all people. They are called to practice life giving; the responsibility for a growth response is between those resisting and God.

Group growth parallels human growth. The stages of group development resemble the stages through which every person moves. As infants we are totally dependent. Later, the child begins to test this dependence and to determine limits of freedom. There are urges for freedom and yet desires for boundaries during adolescent years. At some point, most people break away and test their independence. Then they desire, and feel greater freedom, to renegotiate their relationships based on interdependency—as adult to adult.

Establishing a Covenant

A covenant or contract is basic to group life. It is composed of members' expectations regarding the group and, whether expressed or not, governs all interaction.

A covenant is between parties; one person cannot establish a relationship. And, yet, every individual does have some idea of what he wants from others and what he is willing to give in return. Problems arise when what I want and expect from others is not provided.

In a group, problems may be compounded as unexpressed expectations cause the group to function ineffectively or to fail. Members may not have a clear understanding as to why they are together and may have vastly different ideas about their commitments and their future as a group.

It is a fact: when a person's desires (expectations) are not met, he is disappointed and/or frustrated. So the concern of a leader must focus on what members want from a group and what each is willing to contribute. Expectations always exist; it is the role of the leader to guide the group in surfacing, discussing, and establishing a covenant or contract related to these expectations.

Establishing a covenant involves consensus in four areas:

purpose, expectations, leadership, and meetings. Open discussion and planning at inception is the most effective way to begin a group. For groups already formed, a reassessment in these four areas to clarify expectations and to surface any dissatisfactions would be helpful.

Purpose

If the group is formed for a specific purpose, then this should be clearly stated prior to and during the initial meeting. The group's function can be clarified and discussed as people come together, but the basic statement of intent should be announced in order to assure that only those with compatible expectations come together.

For groups that come together for a vague or unstated purpose, this should be a major agenda item for the first meeting. If a majority of persons decide merely to provide a monthly social and coffee opportunity for compatible persons, this should be discussed and agreed upon. Those interested in a formal, weekly Bible study might not want to commit themselves to such a purpose.

Rather than begin with incompatible or unspoken expectations that lead to an unhealthy group experience, open discussion regarding the purpose of the group will enable those who reach consensus to commit themselves; others may choose not to participate. In the long run, all persons will be much happier.

Expectations

Wants and desires are naturally tied in with purpose. A group may have a stated purpose, but it is the expectations of individuals that must be unified in achieving that purpose. Though all members may express support for a group's stated purpose, there may be varying understandings and commitments regarding the means for accomplishment. A consensus of expectations will alleviate a potential source of conflict.

After everyone has a clear understanding of the group's purpose, the leader will help members focus on questions such as:

- What do you hope to contribute to and gain from the group?
- What personal support are you willing to give others? to give yourself?
- What is the common ground among members' expectations?

It would be helpful to have someone summarize the hopes of the group. Where are individual hopes similar? Where do they diverge?

Leadership

Although related to expectations, this focus is more on actual style and responsibilities for leadership actions within the group. What are the major job functions that will need to be performed? These may be related specifically to a task for which the group is responsible or may be supportive in nature, such as providing refreshments or keeping records. How will each of these responsibilities be handled?

Will the leader do it all? Will individuals or committees be assigned or elected to make decisions? Will people volunteer? Will a different person handle the same responsibility each week? Each month? What does the leader plan to contribute to the group? How do group members expect to be involved in sharing leadership? These are some of the questions that should be discussed in developing a common understanding regarding leadership.

Meetings

When, where, how long, and how often will group meetings be held are major concerns to members. Decisions related to meetings often involve a change in schedules for participants. Changes affect family, job responsibilities, social life, and such; hence, each person has a vested interest.

The intent of consensus in this area is to assure, within the constraints of the group's purpose, that the needs of the greatest number of people are met. Not only does it provide minimal disruption of each individual's existing schedules, but it increases the potential and motivation for attendance.

A Predetermined Contract

Whenever the purpose and guidelines of a group are partially or completely predetermined, this information should be conveyed in advance. Potential group members deserve the opportunity to assess whether or not they can align their needs and expectations with the stated purpose and guidelines for the group.

Participants may be enlisted for such a group, but they should be informed exactly as to what will be expected and what responsibilities they will have in the group. Persons approached in this way have an opportunity to ratify a covenant rather then develop one. This is perfectly acceptable and often desirable, especially for a short-term, task-oriented group such as a committee enlisted to plan, prepare, and serve a church supper.

The Covenant

Once the above items have been discussed and appropriate agreements made, the group has a covenant or contract. These agreements form the guidelines for group life and will serve as a point of reference whenever evaluation is desired or group cohesion disrupted.

A covenant must not be viewed as unchangeable, however. It is designed to aid the group not control it. As conditions change, such as new members, enlarged purpose, or a new leader, the group will need to reaffirm or renegotiate its covenant.

The level of commitment to a group and its purpose will determine to a great extent the degree of influence the covenant has in members' lives. When commitment is low, regardless of the decisions that have been made, a covenant may be treated casually or even ignored. If group commitment is high, however, group decisions tend to be taken much more seriously.

Consequently, a covenant should be viewed only as a statement of how people desire to be related. It must be a clear, realistic, and accurate statement of how people anticipate working together.

The value in establishing a covenant is that people who are involved in making decisions about how they will commit themselves are more highly motivated, gain greater satisfaction from the group, and are more purpose oriented than people who operate with implied or diffused group understandings.

Pattern for Growth

There are three basic activities necessary for group growth: (1) reflection on that which has been, (2) assessment of the present situation, and (3) projection of the future. Growth is incomplete when any one of these is neglected and can be maximized only when group members are attuned to relationships, feelings, and responsibilities in each area.

Reflection

Every group builds on history. To understand and appreciate the influences—both direct and indirect—gives substance and lends credibility to the present existence and purpose of the group. To detach oneself from history, whether yesterday or many years ago, is to lose identity and problem-solving capacity. The basic perspective is: "What does our experience (or past) teach us about the present?" Or, "How can we profit from our past?"

Assessment

What is happening to us or because of us? As we are able to interpret present experience and evaluate historical influence, we can respond in a manner that becomes increasingly reflective of our true selves—including our needs, wants, and values. Judgment and problem-solving ability improves, and energy that otherwise might be used inefficiently can be channeled into more productive actions.

Assessment is basically human evaluation which is used in present-day decision-making. Although seemingly objective, it may well be based on emotion or any other influence experienced by group members. Whatever has been or currently exists is real and provides information that can be a servant of the present. The important thing is to recognize and accept these influences and their effect on group interaction.

Projection

Planning for the future is the first step to increased spiritual and personal growth. Without a vision or a dream of what you want to be or what you want your group or church to be, there is little motivation to do anything constructive.

Using information obtained through reflection and assessment, a group can begin to envision what they would like to be, do, or stand for. Members can identify the difference between where they are and where they would like to be. Just as in the change process, without identification of a discrepancy, there is no possibility for growth or development.

Projection provides an ongoing means for a group to infuse purpose into activity. Whereas a purpose for the group may have been stated initially, periodic projection enables participants to keep in touch with the directions and actions most appropriate for the situation.

Projection, then, is the focal activity of the pattern for growth. It cannot exist alone, however, and constantly must be updated with new information from current experience. This is not to say a group should live in or for the future; projection is simply the way to provide focus, meaning, and direction for present experience.

5.
Working with People in Groups—II

This chapter presents information and gives guidance in ways to elicit caring, supportive relationships and to develop effective group functioning. The content is designed in the form of activities which can be used with a group or can simply be read. The activities will provide an opportunity for entry into relationships at whatever level is comfortable. Participants thus are enabled to establish and strengthen relationships in a supportive, low-risk manner.

The role of the leader is to present, guide, and participate as appropriate—not to direct. Medium to low control is necessary in order to elicit a high level of participation in these activities.

Building Relationships

Levels of Communication

(The leader will provide the following information prior to introducing the activity.)

There is a way to evaluate relationships in a group by examining communication patterns. There are levels of communication that show us whether we have an on-the-surface or an in-depth relationship with others.

These levels of communication can be described by using an illustration like an inverted cone. At the bottom, representing most of our verbal contact with others, is the *cliché* level.

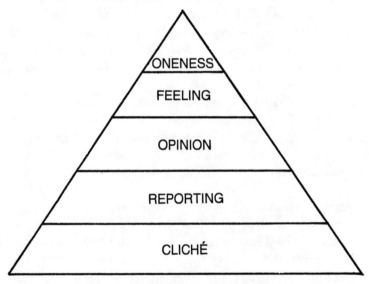

Levels of Communication

This is the foundation for all communication and represents the easy, day-to-day chatter that enables people to move easily among each other in a polite manner. Clichés often heard include: How are you? Nice day. Good morning. Nice to see you. Clichés mean little, and responses, if any, are normally clichés. There is little personal involvement in interacting on this level.

The next level, assuming that people care enough to interact, is *reporting.* This involves giving information or facts. It is basically telling who, what, why, when, or where. Once again, there does not have to be any personal involvement—only an interest in providing or receiving the news.

Opinion or judgment is the third level of communication. This is the first level at which a person begins to reveal something of his real self. I-think or I-believe communications involve risk since others may disagree or may desire to probe your reasoning. This is a give-and-take level when people must for the first time begin to listen to others if communication is to continue.

If trust is present and parties so desire, they may reach the *feeling* level of interpersonal communication. For the first time true caring must be felt. I appreciate you; I love; I hurt; I want to be understood; my goal in life, my needs. . . . Such communication indicates a trusting, caring, supportive relationship.

As the cone in the illustration shows, there are fewer times when we are involved in each of the levels of communication. This also means there are fewer people with whom we interact at each level. Whereas we talk with almost everyone at the cliché level, we interact with relatively few people at the upper levels. This is especially so of the highest level of interaction, which I call *oneness.* This represents those rare moments when we feel totally understood and "at one" with someone else. This communication, not necessarily verbal, indicates a common mind and a feeling of complete understanding. These are those rare moments of human interaction with a few people that can be called peak communication.

Instructions to give: Examine your communication pattern. On a blank sheet, list the five levels and describe some examples you have experienced during the past week. Discuss with several others the patterns you see. At what level were most of your communications? With whom? What was the frequency of communication at the higher levels? With whom or under what circumstances did you reach the feeling and oneness levels? (Allow time for discussion.)

Leader: These reflections help us see the quality of relationships as much as anything. An important thing to remember is that just as in relationships, all communication cannot—and certainly should not—be focused on the higher, intense levels.

We cannot interact on an in-depth level at all times with all people; communication, for emotional and physical well-being, must follow the illustration of the inverted cone. We should be able to communicate on any level depending on the people and situation, the relationships, and the degree of trust.

Problems arise when persons are attempting to communicate with each other but are operating at different levels. For instance, a person might start telling about an illness in response to the question, "How are you?" If the other person intended only to pass a cliché or two, there is potential for frustration. To avoid tension and to maximize understanding, parties involved must match levels of communication. You and I may begin a conversation with clichés, then move on to the other levels. We can relate most effectively if we can sense the movement and match each other at the appropriate level.

Follow-up Activity: Discuss perceptions related to communication in your group, in your family. What is the most dissatisfying part of your communication with others? The most satisfying? How could your group improve its communication?

Communication Styles

There are four general communication styles, each of which exhibits several characteristics. By understanding these and the underlying assumptions, a person can assess his own style or styles and seek ways to be more effective.

Leader: Give the above information, then write on the chalkboard:

Pleaser
Controller
Avoider
Life Giver

Distribute work sheets like the one shown on the following page (Improving Communication). Review and discuss each style of communication; ask persons to match one of the styles listed on the chalkboard with each description. What observations can you make about each style? How does each style affect you? Discuss the values of the life-giver approach. How can this be encouraged?

Body Language

What do we say with body language such as a smile? A frown? An uninterested posture? Try sending some nonverbal messages and see if or how they are interpreted. When are nonverbal messages easy to interpret? When are they most difficult? What messages are encouraging? Discouraging? Do you ever keep reading a newspaper when someone is talking to you? What are you communicating? What is the other person communicating? What does our body language say to children?

Affirmation

Divide into pairs with no family members together. Write on the chalkboard:

I am at my best with people when . . . .

Improving Communication

Communication Style: _____
- Avoids interaction
- Assumes nothing can be done
- Neither contributes nor solicits contributions
- Not interested in new approaches
- Not interested in experimentation

Communication Style: _____
- Shifts the burden to the other fellow
- Explores only to fit in with the other person's viewpoint
- Assumes the other person has more to contribute
- Willing to consider alternatives but doesn't probe to develop them
- Makes few contributions of his own ideas

Communication Style: _____
- Assumes that his own ideas and approaches are best
- Tries to impose or sell his own point of view
- Relies heavily on one-way communications
- Is not interested in experimentation
- Does not like to consider alternatives

Communication Style: _____
- Encourages exploration and experimentation
- Willing to contribute ideas, suggestions, etc.
- Doesn't assume that he is right
- Strives for joint understanding of problems and goals
- Encourages two-way communication

Each person will take one minute to tell about yourself by completing this sentence. After you tell about yourself, your partner will summarize what you have said; you will listen to how your partner heard you. Then it will be your partner's turn to tell about himself.

When finished, follow the same procedure with the next two statements:

I am proudest of my ability to . . . .

I identify my talents as . . . .

Spend about five minutes discussing how you perceive each other's strengths. Then return to the large group. Share what you have learned and/or appreciate about each other.

Reflect on the levels of communication involved in this activity. What does this type of activity teach us?

Improving Communication

In light of our discussions, evaluate the effectiveness of each of the following statements. What might actually be communicated by each? How could each be said in a more supportive and life-giving manner?

1. Is that *all* you had to say?
2. In response to your question, the group doesn't become involved in issues such as that.
3. All Christians need to improve their skills in witnessing, so if no one objects, I'll arrange for a study of the unit on outreach.
4. You really should know better, Jane. Christians shouldn't even think about things such as that.
5. I've thought about how our group ought to do this, and I've decided that we should. . . .

Spiritual Graph

Duplicate or ask each person to sketch the football-field type of diagram illustrated. Note the numbers across the top; these indicate years of age for adults. (If using this exercise with young adults or youth, list years in steps of five rather than ten, for example zero, five, ten, fifteen, twenty.)

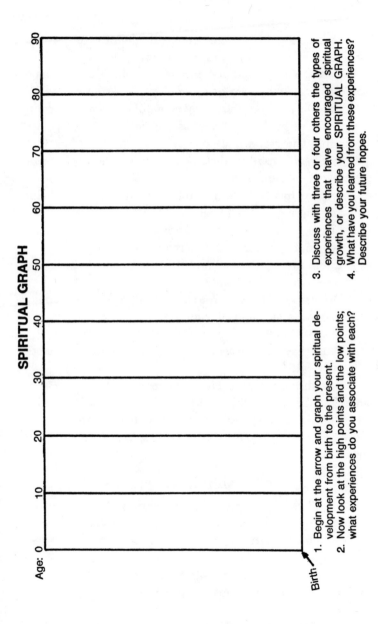

SPIRITUAL GRAPH

Age:

Birth

0   10   20   30   40   50   60   70   80   90

1. Begin at the arrow and graph your spiritual development from birth to the present.

2. Now look at the high points and the low points; what experiences do you associate with each?

3. Discuss with three or four others the types of experiences that have encouraged spiritual growth, or describe your SPIRITUAL GRAPH.

4. What have you learned from these experiences? Describe your future hopes.

If there are eight or more people, divide into groups of four or five; if less than eight, do not divide.

In case some people are unfamiliar with a graph, draw a sample on a chalkboard or sheet of paper. Point out that the line starts at a person's birth (lower left of diagram) and continues to his or her present age (as indicated on the top of the diagram). The graph line goes up or down according to the path a person's spiritual development has taken or the significant events experienced.

Ask participants to do the following (it would be helpful to write these on a chalkboard):

- Begin at the lower left corner and graph your spiritual development from birth to the present.
- Circle the high points and the low points. What experiences do you associate with each?
- Discuss with three or four others the types of experiences that have encouraged your spiritual growth, or describe your spiritual graph as you have drawn it.
- What have you learned from this experience? Describe your future hopes.

When through, participants can return to the large group and describe things they learned about each other. Review the types of experiences that seem to elicit spiritual growth. How can other people help us with spiritual growth? How do we help each other?

Leadership Interventions

There is no substitute for the "being" which a life-giving leader brings to a group. This is the intangible aspect of giving and receiving, initiating and responding based on the felt needs of any situation—without regard to formalized techniques, formulas, or theories of leadership behavior.

However, there are those areas of group life that require

more than simple guidance or support. As problems or potentially unhealthy situations arise, it is the responsibility of the leader to initiate deliberate actions designed to protect the integrity and the purpose of the group, as well as to insure the growth potential for all involved.

Such actions are termed leadership interventions. They are preventive or prescriptive steps taken by a leader to direct or redirect group activity to solve a problem which the leader— and perhaps not the group—perceives.

Listed below are some common interventions practiced by life-giving leaders. Understanding and using them does not assure life-giving results; however, one's problem-solving capacity is in direct proportion to his ability to draw from and effectively use appropriate interventions. Thus, it would be helpful to examine and try out some of these actions at appropriate times. Discover those that you can use effectively and determine the circumstances most effective for each.

Group Decision-Making

The two most useful tools in decision-making are problem-solving and consensus. Each of these is designed to lead people to an accurate and agreeable solution to common problems. They may be used separately as needed but become most effective when used to complement each other in the normal course dealing with group problems.

By mastering the principles of each, these tools can become a normal part of the group process skills of members and of leadership. Here are guidelines for using these methods.

PROBLEM-SOLVING

- Define and analyze the problem.
- Suggest or find alternatives for solving it.
- Evaluate the alternatives.

- Select the alternative that seems most appropriate for solving the problem and try it.
- If the solution is not satisfactory, repeat the process, using the information gained.

CONSENSUS

- Decisions must reflect the general agreement among group members. Work for the best solution, not your solution.
- Avoid arguing for your own individual judgments. Approach the task on the basis of logic.
- Avoid changing your mind only in order to reach agreement and to avoid conflict. Support only solutions with which you are able to agree somewhat.
- Avoid conflict-reducing techniques, such as majority vote and averaging, in reaching your decision.
- View differences of opinion as helpful rather than as a hindrance in decision-making.

Intervention Guidelines for Teachers and Group Leaders

1. If you are responsible for guiding the discussion, follow your plan but be open to adjustments depending on the needs of group members. Occasionally you may feel you are losing control when many people get into the discussion or when several members seem to "chase a rabbit." Resist the impulse to take charge and bring everyone back to the subject. Listen carefully and analyze the situation; members may be involved in a learning or sharing experience growing out of the discussion that is very meaningful to them. When appropriate, make a transitional statement and proceed with your plans.
2. When a person is dominating the discussion, bring other

members in by saying something such as, "John has shared his opinion; what are some other viewpoints?"

3. Whenever disagreement is apparent in a group, lead members to focus on the problem or issue rather than on the people or personalities involved. For example, say, "Let's stop a minute and examine the problem; what is the issue with which we are dealing?"

4. Use the problem-solving process whenever you or the group are stuck in an uncomfortable or unsure situation.

5. If the session becomes disrupted, simply say something like, "I'm a bit uncomfortable about what is happening; how do you feel about it?" Evaluate, regroup, and then proceed.

   NOTE: If the disruption is potentially embarrassing to someone, a different approach is needed. Seek to put the person at ease rather than leading the group to evaluate the situation. (This *may* include ignoring the disruption.) Proceed when appropriate.

6. In the case of a crucial problem that is particularly disrupting, consider using the problem-solving process. If necessary, save the planned session for another meeting.

7. Call for information, clarification, elaboration, or summary whenever appropriate. Do not assume that everyone is staying with the trend of thought and that the major points will be recognized. Involve group members by saying things such as:

   • Does someone have additional information on this?
   • Bill, will you please clarify your earlier statement?
   • Linda, talk a little bit more about that; how did you get it started?
   • Lynne, would you summarize the main points that have been made?

8. Value the contribution of every person. A comment may seem to be off the subject to you, but it could be the best thought a person has had during the session and perhaps very important to him or even to the group. Sometimes, however, a person may become an overactive participant and restrict the participation of others. In this case, you might say tactfully, "Okay, now let's hear what others have to say," or "Thank you; what do the rest of you think?"

9. Avoid speaking for the group unless you have been authorized to do so. Some leaders make the mistake of saying to the group things such as, "Of course, everyone in our group already is in favor of this." If this is not a fact, then this type of statement creates hostility or tension in those who disagree. A better approach would be to say, "Some may already favor this." The best procedure to follow if participation is appropriate is to let people speak for themselves.

10. Involve group members in making decisions that will affect them. This indicates that in the leader's opinion the group is important and that the contributions of each person are valued. Another benefit is that members have a stronger commitment to carry out decisions which they have helped to make.

11. Affirm and encourage the worthy contributions of members. Give praise when due and avoid blaming when things go wrong. Affirmation and praise encourage growth and participation. Blaming stifles growth.

Assessment of Group Member Roles

This is a group activity designed to involve members in assessing and in diagnosing appropriate ways to improve their group life. Whereas the leader could do this assessment, implementing appropriate changes within the group would be rather difficult. However, if members identify discrepancies themselves, they will likely work to improve any shortcomings.

On the next page is a list and descriptions of common roles performed by group members. This can be duplicated and distributed.

Ask members to read the descriptions of the various roles played by persons in a group. Point out that each person fulfills a variety of roles, depending on the situation; but each of us becomes associated with a few dominant ones. No person can fill all of the roles; that is one reason a group can be so meaningful and often achieve more than individuals.

Note that there are three general categories: Task Roles, Growing and Vitalizing Roles, and Blocking/Hindering Roles. The first two are vital to the life of a group and must be performed regularly. The third category represents behavior that interferes with group interaction.

Also illustrated (p. 92) is a work sheet; pass out duplicated copies. Divide into groups of eight or less and ask each to pull into a small circle. Give the following instructions:

- On the work sheet (p. 92), write your name next to #1. Pass the sheets around the circle so that each person can write his name on each sheet. You should end up with your own sheet.
- Listed at the top of the work sheet are the various roles. For each person, including yourself, place at least two checks and not more than five checks under the roles which that person has filled rather consistently while a member of the group. Do this without discussion, please.

(After sheets have been checked, continue.)

- Now share with those in your group what you checked

Group Member Roles

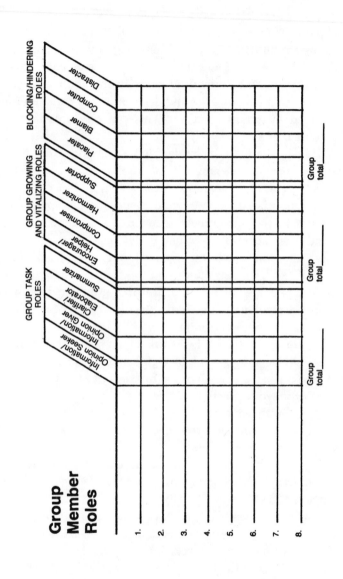

	GROUP TASK ROLES				GROUP GROWING AND VITALIZING ROLES				BLOCKING/HINDERING ROLES			
	Information/ Opinion Seeker	Information/ Opinion Giver	Clarifier/ Elaborator	Summarizer	Encourager/ Helper	Compromiser	Harmonizer	Supporter	Placater	Blamer	Computer	Distracter
1.												
2.												
3.												
4.												
5.												
6.												
7.												
8.												
	Group total ____				Group total ____				Group total ____			

Group Member Roles

An Exercise in Understanding Group Behavior

—

Bruce P. Powers

Listed below are descriptions of some common group member roles. The leader will provide additional information regarding these roles and give instructions for use of the attached work sheet.

TASK ROLES

Information/Opinion Seeker—Requesting facts or expressions of feeling; seeking information or suggestions and ideas related to group concerns.

Information/Opinion Giver—Providing facts or relevant information; sharing beliefs, suggestions, and ideas related to group concerns.

Classifier/Elaborator—Interpreting ideas or suggestions; indicating alternatives and issues before the group; giving examples and developing meanings.

Summarizer—Pulling together related ideas; describing the trend of group thinking.

GROWING AND VITALIZING ROLES

Encourager/Helper—Being friendly, warm, and responsive to others; assisting and affirming fellow group members.

Compromiser—Giving ground when one's ideas, status, or actions are in conflict with those of one or more group members.

Harmonizer—Attempting to reconcile disagreements; getting people to explore their differences.

Supporter—Accepting and giving support to group decisions and actions.

BLOCKING/HINDERING ROLES

Placater—Subordinating self to others.

Blamer—Judging others to be at fault.

Computer—Calculating answers without regard to emotion or other variables.

Distracter—Calling attention to something off the subject; leading the group astray.

for each person, including yourself, and why. Ask for information on your own actions. Explore differences on various sheets.

(Allow time for discussion.)

• Here are some insights that might make this exercise more meaningful. Count the total number of checks in each category and total them for your group. There should be a fairly close score for the first two categories and a low score for the third. (If there are two or more subgroups, also total for the entire group.)

The importance of this type evaluation is to help members see whether they are complementing each other or whether they are operating as self-centered persons. It is important to share in filling the roles in the first two categories and to seek individually to eliminate behavior in the third category.

To conclude this exercise, discuss what members discovered and how this may affect group behavior. Other applications and implications of the activity will arise. Discuss and explore opportunities for improvement.

Looking Ahead

On the next page is a work sheet for a process-oriented activity that focuses on personal evaluation and projection. The essential elements are identifying personal goals, determining the factors that would help achieve those goals, and acknowledging the personal strengths and limitations involved.

This is an individual activity but can be pursued very effectively in groups by having three or four persons discuss their answers with each other. Then pursue a group discussion on personal goals, the meaning of the activity, and things learned.

By a simple adjustment of words, this activity also can be

Looking Ahead

1. Describe in twenty-five words or less the type of person you would like to be five years from now. Discuss.

2. What factors will help to make this happen?

What stands in the way of accomplishing this?

3. Strengths on which I need to build:

Limitations with which I need to deal:

4. Share the above with a friend. Discuss opportunities for growth.

used for group projection: substitute group for person, and we for I.

How Are We Doing?

Here is an informal method of evaluation. As someone records responses on a poster or chalkboard, ask group members to call out the first word that comes to mind when you ask the following question: How do you feel about our group so far?

After the words have been listed, ask members why they chose the words. Discuss members' reactions to the group thus far.

Be open to positive and to negative responses. Explore ways to improve any shortcomings. Describe the value of periodic evaluation and ask members what they think. Discuss any new insights and summarize the feelings expressed.

How Did We Do?

A more formal evaluation is often desired, particularly at the conclusion of a series of meetings. By using an instrument such as the "Small Group Evaluation Sheet," participants can list their reactions in six key areas, plus add any pertinent comments or suggestions.

Responses can be compiled and a summary report prepared indicating the degree of success in each area. Comments and suggestions can be received for general tendencies and priority established for subsequent group and/or leadership involvement.

Summary

Relational needs are perhaps the strongest influence on evangelical Christians. Not only are interpersonal support systems

SMALL-GROUP EVALUATION SHEET

Give your honest and immediate impression in response to the following items by placing an *X* at the appropriate place on each line.

1. Leadership was:

/_____/_____/_____/_____/_____/

Dominated by   Shared by all
one person   members of the group

2. Communication was:

/_____/_____/_____/_____/_____/

Very   Very open
Difficult   and free-flowing

3. People were:

/_____/_____/_____/_____/_____/

Phony   Honest and
                                              authentic

4. The group was:

/_____/_____/_____/_____/_____/

Avoiding   Working hard
its task   at its task

5. I felt:

/_____/_____/_____/_____/_____/

Misunderstood   Completely accepted
and rejected   and understood

6. I rate the overall value of my group experience:

/_____/_____/_____/_____/_____/

Insignificant   Significant

Additional comments and/or suggestions:

necessary in fulfilling each Christian's call to mission, but such relationships are essential to our being the body of Christ to the world.

A life-giving leader must understand this need and be committed to its fulfillment in a manner that will find greatest expression in Christian growth and service.

The understandings and techniques presented in this chapter will assist the Christian leader in creating an environment conducive to such development. In the end, however, it is not the leader, and it is not the people; it is God who enables and, in his own way, uses the group environment and the commitment of his people to empower them for growth and service.

6.
Leadership and the Will of God

Several days before Martin Luther King was murdered, he said in a speech: "I don't know what will happen now. We've got some difficult days ahead. But it really doesn't matter to me now, because I've been to the mountaintop. I won't mind. I just want to do God's will." [1] In response to his death, his wife said that it was God's will.

What *is* God's will? How does a leader determine the will of God for his life or for those with whom he works? These are perplexing questions for those who are honest enough to question and secure enough to search.

During the latter 1960's, a religious-emphasis-week speaker on a Baptist college campus suggested to the student body that there ought to be a thirty-year moratorium on the use of the term "God's will." The problem, he suggested, is that we often pervert the concept of following God's will and in reality use God to legitimize whatever we desire.

This is a biting accusation, but who has not heard such examples: I feel it is God's will for me to change jobs, get married, buy a house, take a trip, avoid military service . . . and there are also attempts to explain circumstances by invoking God's will: It was God's will that my loved one contracted cancer, that the tornado destroyed the town, that our business was successful, that I survived the plane crash. . . .

When we say, "Thy will be done," just what do we mean? When we commit ourselves to follow Jesus, just what are our intentions? How *does* a person determine the will of God?

The Wrong Emphasis

Many of the problems faced in interpreting God's will arise because of a misplaced emphasis. Whereas God has provided general guidance for fulfilling his will, many people seek the security of specific instructions. Rather than basing their lives on principles and guidelines (and accepting personal responsibility for their actions) they feel it necessary to explain every action or circumstance by attributing it to God's will.

Aside from specific revelations, God appears to have given to his highest creation the guidelines and the ability to live within his will. Rather than creating and guiding puppets, God has chosen to provide man with the freedom and the responsibility to determine the specific applications of his will. Were this the major thrust of the chapter, appropriate support might be expected. But suffice it to say: a person seeking the will of God is ultimately involved in making a human decision whether or not something is indeed the will of God. The emphasis in the teachings of Jesus is clearly on the personal responsibility of believers to live within the guidelines he taught rather than conform to the "letter of the law."

Living God's Will

The principles and guidelines for living God's will are the same ones that undergird the life-giving approach to Christian leadership. The style is that of a pilgrim follower, always striving to live in the image of Christ but never quite able.

In my own pilgrimage, I have accepted the fact that I will always be in the process of doing and being God's will rather than "discovering" it. This is not—and has not been—easy; I want as much as anyone to find God's will for my life, get within his will, and settle down to live my religion. As a leader, I have always wanted to lead people to do the same.

In seeking to understand God's will both in my personal life and among the people with whom I work, I had a unique experience which brought to light a key to interpreting God's will for individuals and for groups of Christians.

As mentioned in an earlier chapter, New Testament teachings regarding spiritual gifts represent one way of understanding God's will for our lives. I believe this to be the key concept for leaders to follow in seeking to help Christians understand, interpret, and practice God's will.

God's Gifts

During the summer of 1972, I had an experience that has become a stack pole for this concept of Christian leadership. I want to share it with you in the hope that it will give additional insight to understanding and practicing God's will both for yourself and those whom you seek to lead.

I described earlier my struggle to understand Jesus' teachings related to leadership. As an outgrowth of this, I began to focus on what became a question of integrity for me: What am I doing to people? I felt called by God to be a church staff member, to guide churches in understanding and applying the gospel of Jesus Christ.

But what about the calling of church members? Did I have all the insight and better contact with God than they? What about the differing interpretations among members about what was God's will for our church? When the congregation looked to me for guidance, what right did I have to detail God's will for our church?

This concern had just begun to surface when I was contacted about serving in a denominational leadership position. As I sought to make a decision, the question kept returning: What would I be doing to people? And, would this be within God's will both for those whom I would lead and for my own life?

Finally, I had to admit to myself that I could not serve in such a position with the unresolved questions. It would not be fair to the denominational agency, to the people in the churches, or to me.

I turned down the offer by saying that I just didn't feel right about it. Then I prayed to God that I had made the right decision; if they couldn't find the appropriate person and came back to me in the future, I would take this as indication that I should give more serious consideration to the offer.

Four months passed without contact. Then a call came that they still felt I was the person for the position. After intense personal deliberation, I finally told them that I would accept if they would be patient with me and let me bring myself as I was, struggles and all.

For over a year, I quietly filled the role of one who knows what is best for the churches. Many people listened; but some people questioned. And quite often the questions were the same ones that had been bothering me, about what is God's will . . . for my church, for me, for my Sunday School class, for my mission group, and such.

Finally, I decided that I was going to explore this problem with people as honestly as possible; I was at appropriate times going to discuss my struggles and commitments and ask them to join me in seeking to understand God's will.

This decision came just prior to six, one-week leadership

conferences I was to lead at Glorieta and at Ridgecrest Baptist conference centers during the summer of 1972. I designed the agendas for these meetings so that all who so desired could work together on this problem.

With seventy-five to one hundred leaders in each conference, I shared the idea for us working together to understand how God's will is interpreted through leadership. The response was enthusiastic. People said that for the first time, many of them were hearing someone in a denominational leadership position acting, speaking, and feeling as they do.

The participants were pleased, but from my perspective not much emerged during the first two conferences. People seemed preoccupied with using theological-sounding words and long, complicated phrases with each other to describe and interpret their understandings. I thought to myself that perhaps we're getting the right words and praying and saying the right phrases, but there is something missing.

On the last day of the third conference, it came time for a small group that had intently been seeking answers to the function of leadership to report. This elderly gentleman stood and said to the conference, "I'm almost ashamed to share with you what our group has to report, for it is so simple it sounds like a kid's language." After some friendly encouragement from persons nearby, he said, "Now here's what our group feels the role of leadership is in the church. It is to equip Christians to *be,* to *do,* and to *tell* the gospel."

In the midst of all the lengthy and complicated statements, this was a simple, beautiful description that anyone could understand. For a long moment, the conference was quiet as we all reflected on the significance of this statement. For me, this was the highlight of the first three conferences. But how did God intend for leaders to do this?

I tried not to think about it, but my mind kept working

during four days of driving to Ridgecrest, North Carolina. Then for two weeks, the same struggle. Every afternoon I sat out on a porch overlooking the mountains to review plans for the next day and to ponder what I had been experiencing.

One day I was trying to organize information and experiences of the four previous leadership conferences when I had what I consider a revelation. I realized for the first time that there were four things which I had been believing all my Christian life that, if I put them together, I would have an answer about the role of the leader in God's will. So let me share these four things with you; then I want to tell what I think they mean.

First, God is the Creator and Sustainer of the universe and all that is in it.

Second, there is purpose in all creation. Thinking back on this statement, I recall during that particular week at Ridgecrest that Grady Nutt had been speaking to the youth conference. The kids were impressed by Grady's affirmation that "God don't make no junk! You are a person of worth." This played on my mind and, although the language isn't so good, it helped focus my thoughts on the significant influence God exerts in creation.

The third thing I realized was that Christians as the people of God and the body of Christ—these are the two primary concepts of the church in the New Testament—have the same mission to the world as did God in Christ. As the church, we are to function as the people of God and the body of Christ in seeking to redeem the world.

Fourth, Christians have been endowed with gifts which are to be discovered, developed, and used in carrying out God's mission. Time and again, the New Testament focuses on this concept. If we take these teachings seriously (and I do), every believer possesses a gift or gifts to be used in Christian service.

These are four basic teachings that I had studied many times. But as I put them together that afternoon, it came to me that if I *really* believed them, there was something that followed that I must also believe. And if so, here was my answer to the role of leadership in understanding and interpreting God's will:

A local church brought into being, or created, in response to God's leadership possesses in some form all the gifts—that is talents, abilities, skills, and other resources—which are essential for that body of believers to carry out their portion of God's mission in their particular area.

Now let me say this a little differently. If God has truly called a local congregation together, no matter how big or how small, and we believe these four things I mentioned to you, must we not also believe that God in his wisdom has given to those people whatever gifts might be necessary for their particular time and place?

Here is the key to understanding God's will for leadership and for the church. Rather than seeking specific guidance, God's will is more directly related to discovering, developing, and using the gifts which we have been given.

We have been expecting God to control completely our lives and service. But this does not seem to be his desire. Rather he bestows gifts on his people and calls them to service. Being involved in the discovery, development, and use of spiritual gifts is being within God's will.

As for leadership, our role is two-fold: to involve individuals in discovering, developing, and using their gifts and to assist groups or congregations in eliciting, combining, and directing the use of gifts in appropriate Christian service.

Granted, there are many other positions that could be taken

regarding God's will, but this is the one that has been most helpful to me. I acknowledge the necessity for cooperative relationships among churches such as associations, conventions, and such. Through these larger groupings of the church we are enabled to combine gifts to perform many ministries not possible by one congregation. I also realize that there is often an imbalance in population or economic patterns that dictates support of weak churches or missions. No local congregation is self-sufficient nor has it responsibility for the total mission of the church. However, as more churches combine their resources, they become capable of accepting a greater responsibility for the total mission of the church.

Full expression of my life or a church's life can be found by seeking to *be, do,* and *tell* the gospel. This is the purpose we must be about as Christians; and the process that represents God's will for achieving this purpose is the continual discovery, development, and use of the spiritual gifts imparted to us.

Discovering and Developing Spiritual Gifts

Although this is presented simply as one person's testimony, I would be remiss if I did not recount some of the insights gained since that experience. Time has reinforced and broadened my commitment to the equipping-enabling role of a leader; and a continual effort to be involved in the process myself has been richly rewarding. Consequently, I have included an activity-oriented section for those who would like to know more about or pursue personal development related to spiritual gifts.

Biblical Foundations

Listed below are some of the key New Testament passages regarding spiritual gifts. After reading each, review the comments I have made, then recheck the Scripture passage to clarify your own understanding.

Romans 12:4–8

There are three prominent concepts in this passage: Although many, we are to function as one body; we possess a variety of gifts; and we are to use the gifts which God has given.

1 Corinthians 12:4–11

Along with differing gifts, there are different ways of using or expressing those gifts; however, God is the source of and sustainer in the use of all spiritual gifts. There may be differences in ability, but everyone is given some gift to use in Christian service. Verse 7 is important: To each is given for the common good or for the good of all. Spiritual gifts are not personal; they must find expression either in building the Christian body or in service on behalf of the body.

Ephesians 4:11–13

Gifts are provided to equip all God's people for Christian service and to build up the body of Christ. Through the use of spiritual gifts we move toward the Christian ideal: oneness in faith and in knowledge of and commitment to Jesus Christ. The growth expectation is explicit in this passage; we are to seek maturity in the likeness of Christ.

1 Peter 4:10–11

The emphasis in this passage is on the use of God's gifts for the good of others.

Implications

In reflecting on these Scripture passages, consider the following as implications:

• Gifts may be latent, undiscovered, or underdeveloped; however, every Christian possesses one or more.

• Activity that does not build the body or find expression in Christian service does not represent a spiritual gift.

• Spiritual gifts must be affirmed by others; we cannot adequately judge our personal effectiveness or determine our possession of a spiritual gift.

• God's Spirit guides, but it is the responsibility of every Christian to develop and use his gifts.

• Gifts and the ability to use them may vary depending on the Spirit's guidance. Once a gift is developed and used does not necessarily mean that it will be the dominant or only one to be used throughout a person's life. Depending on the situation, God may call forth any variety of gifts.

• Personal skills and abilities may or may not be spiritual gifts. The test is: Are they affirmed by others as building the body and are they useful in Christian service?

• God will bless the use of his gifts.

• The gifts of one person will be supportive of and not in conflict with the gifts of others in the body.

• Christian service within and outside the body is much more effective and rewarding if persons are operating out of a gift motivation.

• The use of spiritual gifts will engender positive feelings and responses among members of the body.

Categories of Spiritual Gifts

What are the types of gifts mentioned in the New Testament and affirmed through Christian history and experience? In a study kit on spiritual gifts, *Nexus:* (see Resources), four general areas of gifts are suggested. Each of these areas is then further divided into categories of spiritual gifts. The premise is that the discovering of gifts proceeds from a general recognition and affirmation to a category, then to a specific expression.

Listed below are areas and categories of gifts that might be included. You may want to reflect on your experience in each of the categories and perhaps identify some additional types or specific expressions of gifts that might be included.

Gift Area	*Categories*
Fellowship and Group Life	Service
	Fellowship
	Administration
	Stewardship
Nurturing Others	Teaching
	Shepherding
	Healing
	Preaching
Ministry in the World	Evangelism
	Reconciliation
	Ministry/Service
	Prophecy
Inner Life of the Spirit	Faith/Prayer
	Special Powers
	Wisdom/Knowledge/Discernment
	Worship

Guidelines for Discovery and Development

Here are some guidelines I have used in my own life and in retreats and leadership seminars to help participants focus on the gifts they possess.

List your strengths. Include the things you enjoy doing the most. When are you at your best? What things would you rather be doing than anything else? Review this list and see what patterns develop. Are there some areas of strength and/or interest that you have been able to use effectively in Christian service where they have been affirmed by fellow Christians?

Affirm and be affirmed. This is the natural process that supports the discovery and development of spiritual gifts. One of the most helpful ways you can assist me is by affirming the actions, interests, and abilities that contribute significantly to your spiritual development; and I can do the same for you. As Christians interact, they have opportunity to observe and experience each other in a variety of situations. The gifts that emerge under such conditions should be affirmed, encouraged, and examined for further use and development.

Discover what effect you have on others. Spiritual gifts cause something desirable to happen in others. You must ask yourself, "What do I cause to happen?" Reflect on your personal experience and seek the guidance of persons who know you well and obviously care for you. When and under what conditions are you most effective with individuals? With groups? In Christian service?

The importance of this type of introspection can be seen in the example of a Sunday School teacher who thinks that she is using her gift. Unless she causes something positive to happen among class members—in the opinion of those she teaches—she might rightly question whether teaching is her particular gift.

Another approach is to solicit additional feedback when someone affirms you. Ask for more information and if possible, explore with the person whether or not this is a first or one-time impression and under what circumstances you and/or others have elicited similar feelings. How do *you* feel about the action or ability that was affirmed? Has this happened before under similar circumstances? If so, evaluate the circumstances and determine the influences that were operating.

Try on gifts. As you become aware of potential or undeveloped gifts, try them out. Learn about them, practice them, and see how they feel. What do they cause to happen in you? In others? The best way to test gifts is to try them. But don't expect to start with a fully developed gift. The degree of ability varies as well as the level of maturity in utilizing a gift.

Gifts are presents from God that must be discovered, developed, and used. They are not given indiscriminately for people to use or abuse as they see fit; but they are given to be evoked and refined among a caring, sharing, and supportive body of Christians. If a gift is rightly yours, you will come to know it; if not, continue to search.

Constantly search for the meaning of your gifts. Through prayer, study, discussion, and personal reflection you can seek out additional insights and guidance about your gifts. Explore all of the richness of your personal feelings and the reactions of fellow Christians. Monitor the pace and activity in your own life; what story is it telling?

Gordon Cosby, a pastor in Washington, D.C., often describes how he tunes in on his own feelings related to gifts. There are three things he looks for in spiritual gifts: (1) A feeling of "eureka!" (2) talking about it all the time, and (3) can't help but do it.

Build on gifts. God provides a diversity of gifts in varying degrees of ability. There is no expectation that any one Christian will be involved or be equipped to serve in all areas. The implication is that Christians are to focus on the development and use of gifts they possess; they are not to be all things to all people.

One of the guidelines in *Nexus* suggests that many people are timid and cautious at first in attempting to discover and develop their gifts: "In discovering your gifts you find the will of God for your life, and God always wills the best for you. You are not being selfish in searching for your gifts. They are not for you; they are for others. Gift discovery is a lifetime process. Be willing to share the workings of the spirit in your life" (pp. 4–5).

Focus your time and energy on ministering and serving through your gifts. Place yourself in situations and accept assignments where you will be operating out of gift rather than "oughtness." You will experience satisfaction and be living within God's will when building on your gifts.

Do not be afraid of failure. Failure not only helps us discover and refine gifts, it also provides valuable insights that will contribute to more effective functioning at a later date. And, remember, we are called to *practice* our gifts; we must not seek our reward in the results so much as in performing our gifts with quality and integrity. The final result is in God's hands— between God and those to whom we minister.

Accountability and Responsibility

The accountability for stewardship of gifts is to God. Temporal judgments, while they may influence the development and use of gifts, are insignificant compared to the responsibility to one's Creator and Lord. I am convinced that final judgment will in some way consider the degree to which each Christian has developed and used his gifts.

Responsibility for spiritual gifts is more diverse, however— most specifically to self, fellow Christians, and to the local congregation of which one is a part. I must acknowledge and practice the gifts I possess and assume related leadership responsibilities; it is the responsibility of others to affirm and respond to my leadership. At the point of others' gifts, I must respond in a like manner. (This relates specifically to the action-reaction pattern presented in chapter 1.)

Gifts must be practiced with and through other Christians

and the local body of which one is a part. This is not only a responsibility but also a requirement for the effective functioning of the Christian body.

I am also responsible for affirming gifts in others and allowing myself to be affirmed. This is an ongoing process that recognizes dynamic movement of God among us to evoke and channel gifts as appropriate to fulfill his mission. Gifts and calling may change, and Christians must be quick to respond and to assist and support others in determining God's will for their lives.

Where to from Here?

The life-giving approach to leadership is more caught up in being, in process, in relationships than in achieving or discovering an end. So it must be with spiritual gifts; the means are more important than any goal or reward which we may identify.

God does not promise that we will *achieve* his mission; our responsibility is implementation—to *be, do,* and *tell* the gospel. We are not to judge the results; that is up to God.

In all of this, spiritual gifts must be viewed as an integral part and expression of life-giving leadership. They represent a lifetime involvement in discovery, growth, and practice and, in turn, provide satisfaction and service within God's will.

---

[1] Coretta Scott King, *My Life with Martin Luther King, Jr.* (New York: Holt, Rinehart & Winston, Inc., 1969), p. 316.

7.
Toward Full Maturity

In a sense, this closing chapter is a send-off to continual growth—spiritually, mentally, emotionally, relationally, in fact in every way that enables one to be a life-giving leader. Rather than being an action plan, however, it is an overview of the type of environment, personal qualities, and values that provide potential for growth and self-actualization. No one can tell you or me how to grow; such is a unique and personal pilgrimage which each of us must discover and pursue for ourselves. But awareness of factors that encourage and elicit growth does provide options which each person may evaluate and incorporate as appropriate.

Concept of Growth

Growth must be seen from two perspectives: individual and corporate. As pointed out earlier, every Christian is called to become all that he is capable of being as a child of God. This struggle for discovery, development, and fulfillment is very personal yet dependent on a loving, supportive community of faith which will nurture and support the growth process.

The individual perspective of growth may seem self-centered

or selfish in nature, but without love of and concern for self, there is little likelihood that a person can effectively share love with others. Concern for individual growth, therefore, must come first; but to be complete, this concern must be complemented with a commitment to corporate growth.

Corporate growth relates to the spiritual growth of a group or congregation; to the development of a nurturing, caring, cohesive body; to the process of discovering, developing, and using spiritual gifts; to the reaching of the multitudes for Jesus Christ. These are part of that which corporate growth is all about—a small part. Not definable is the greater part, the power or force that continually infuses, renews, refines, and integrates everything that the body is and represents: the Spirit of God.

There are those who dichotomize individual and corporate growth, usually at the point of meeting personal needs *versus* reaching, or evangelizing, the masses. This is unfortunate because neither can be fully accomplished without the other. Each supports the other and makes the other more effective.

Life-giving leaders not only desire growth for themselves but also for the entire body of which they are a part. They value the same opportunity for every person and know that when all are committed to the purpose of God and to each other, God will empower the union with meaning, ability, and substance greater than the sum of the parts.

The Environment: People in Purpose

The environment most conducive to growth is one permeated with purpose, when every action, every structure, every decision reflects the reason for being. There exists in such a milieu a high degree of congruence between surface characteristics and the essence of the organization.

Koinonia, a Greek word used in the New Testament to describe

the church, gives us an idea of what Christians might expect
if they earnestly seek to understand and follow God's will.
Oneness, unity, caring, sharing, supportive fellowship—all are
descriptive of *koinonia,* yet they don't quite capture the gist
implied in the New Testament. Really, the word *koinonia*
suggests that all of these things are possible, but only because
of the presence of something greater than that which the people
involved might represent.

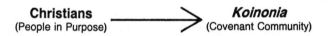

Christians   *Koinonia*
(People in Purpose)   (Covenant Community)

In this diagram, the direction of Christian growth is indicated: toward a state or environment such as that implied by
the word *koinonia.* As indicated on the left, Christians have a
common Lord and common purpose—thus the term, People
in Purpose. However, they are one in the Spirit only because
of their relationship to Jesus Christ; there is no automatic caring, sharing, supportive fellowship among strangers. Only as
they become a community of believers and develop an environment of *koinonia* can Christians understand and appreciate what
it means to be the body of Christ (see Col. 1:18).

Assuming that moving toward *koinonia* is an acceptable direction for Christian growth, how does it happen? how can you
recognize it? and how can you encourage it?

We are prone to assume that such a relationship develops
automatically, that it is simply a by-product of Christian people
being together. But, upon reflection, few of us would try to
explain such a phenomenon so glibly.

In trying to understand how *koinonia* develops, let's look at
another diagram.

As Christians (People in Purpose) come together, they share

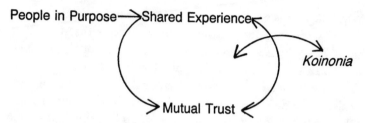

People in Purpose ⟶ Shared Experience

Koinonia

Mutual Trust

many things—study, worship, fellowship, and such. Then an interesting thing happens. As people share experiences together, mutual trust and faith in each other begin to develop. Let me give you an example.

In establishing a friendship you usually have initial experiences such as introductions, handshaking, and small talk. These limited experiences provide an initial exposure which, in a very small way, breaks down barriers between people. This interaction, if satisfying, elicits a slight amount of trust and acceptance between those involved. And more shared experience creates potential for more mutual trust. Thus the friendship intensifies until one person in the relationship ceases to match the other, either in experiences shared or in level of trust. Then the friendship tends to stabilize at that level.

Now let's look at the church. As experiences are shared, people develop a little bit of faith and trust in each other. This creates the potential for more shared experiences. And, as in developing a friendship, the cycle progresses as people experience more things together and gain a greater degree of mutual trust. The difference here is that the growth cycle can continue even if some individuals drop out along the way (as is the case in any congregation). But here is the key: as Christians grow in shared experience and mutual trust, they also are maturing in their faith; this is because who they are and what they do is a reflection of their purpose for being together.

It is sometime during this maturing process that Christians begin to become aware of something that cannot be explained in human terms—*koinonia*. Through the gift of God, Christians find themselves in a growing relationship which in the eyes of the world defies explanation. They become a caring, sharing, supportive group of Christians who can do all things, through Christ, that build his church.

Relating this to leadership, we cannot give people purpose; that is something that comes as a person accepts Jesus Christ as Lord and Savior. Nor can we create and give people *koinonia*—that is a gift from God. But what we can do is encourage and enable Christians to create the potential for *koinonia*—to pursue growth individually and as a body, praying that God will guide and strengthen them as they seek to be his people. Then God in his wisdom will empower and bless to accomplish his purpose.

This, then, is the environment most conducive to growth; and it is also the milieu in which life-giving leadership can make its most significant contributions.

Personal Qualities

Over the years I have come to appreciate qualities in some people that seem to enable them to learn from a great variety of experiences—be they good or bad. These people have an outlook on life that transcends the ordinary. Apparently not hampered by a fear of failure and not controlled by a desire for success, they value every experience simply because they are able to learn about themselves and about their world. As they reflect on and react to various situations in life, they grow.

This does not mean that a person floats about, pushed by

every wave; rather in all experiences both intended and coincidental—one is able to find meaning that enables him to become a more complete or more mature individual. Christians, indeed, are urged to "Rejoice always, pray constantly, give thanks in all circumstances; for this is the will of God in Christ Jesus for you" (1 Thess. 5:16–18, RSV). But what qualities enable a person to hold such an outlook on life?

I was helped in identifying these qualities while attending a marriage enrichment retreat led by author-teacher Reuel Howe. He described his struggle to understand the direction of growth and how various personal and community factors influence the extent and the meaning of all experiences. Let me describe some of his insights and the ideas he spawned in my mind.

Illustrated below is a lifeline. It begins on the left at the

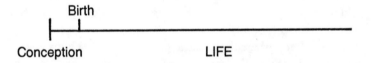

point of conception and continues to the right, not toward death but toward *life*—or toward full maturity in Jesus Christ.

While in the womb, the fetus is comfortable and secure, growing toward independence from the mother's body. At birth, the infant enters the world to new experiences and for the first time must begin to seek satisfaction for basic needs.

The young child is usually fortunate and has great success in meeting his needs. He learns to wiggle, to crawl, to walk, to run, to cry, to babble, to speak words and, later, sentences. In essence, he begins to master his world, partly because of those who care for him and partly due to maturation. And so life develops.

But a strange thing begins to happen to the child and to the youth and to the young adult. Those built-in, protected chances for successful growth and development occur less and less frequently. And the potential for failure—and consequent pain—increases inversely.

Whereas a child *will* learn to walk, to talk, and to control his bowel movements, there are no such future guarantees as a person gradually moves into a life in which success is not assured. During this transition, a person comes to see that in every new experience the potential for pain is as real as for pleasure. Thus, as a part of this process, the qualities begin to emerge that determine one's lifelong stance toward growth.

As a person becomes involved in new experiences, he seeks success (pleasure) and avoids failure (pain). When young, due to a predominance of success, a child ventures into many new experiences. But he becomes wary of pain, and as he grows older, he becomes wiser; that is, he avoids doing things that might lead to failure.

Here, then, particularly as a person leaves school, settles down, and escapes the demands of having to face new experiences, comes the point of escape. Rather than continue growing toward *life*—and risking pain as well as pleasure—some people retreat to a womb-like existence. By risking little in terms of new experiences, they feel secure—like a fetus in its mother.

But such a life-style not only restricts growth, it also assures that a person cannot fulfill the biblical expectation that Christians are to worship, to witness, to minister, and to teach regardless of the consequences.

Now, I am not suggesting that Christians who value growth lack feeling, that they can experience failure but not hurt. This just isn't so. However, the process of growth must be viewed as shown below, where the growth toward life is more a series

of advances and retreats, successes and failures, pleasure and pain. Always, the risk of growth is faced not just for the success that might be achieved but for the value that accrues in trying to become all that one is capable of becoming as a child of God.

Thus, success is desirable but not necessary, and failure is always a possibility. The value is in the growth that occurs, regardless of the outcome. And the direction of personal experience, though it may have setbacks, is always toward *life*.

The personal qualities that evolve in this process may be viewed as characteristics a person exhibits when moving either toward life or toward the "womb." Here are some easily observed examples:

Toward Womb←————**Personal Characteristics**————→**Toward Life**

Closed stance	Open stance
Opaque self	Transparent self
Other controlled	Self-controlled
Past/Future oriented	Present oriented
Preserving	Transforming
Over-rational	Emotionally honest
Ends justify means	Means consonant with ends
Formal education	Lifelong learning
"Ought" commitment	"Want" commitment

The person moving toward life will in general value and exemplify the characteristics listed on the right. This does not mean the person has achieved, or will ever achieve, the end represented by the characteristics. But the progression generally is away from the womb-type traits toward the qualities listed under *life*. This is a journey, with successes and failures, advances and retreats, attempted to achieve a fuller expression of the values held by the life-giving and life-seeking leader.

Let me describe in very broad terms a life-seeking person.

Open stance *vs.* Closed stance—This refers primarily to outlook on life. The life-seeking person tends to be open to new experiences, ideas, and directions. He is a tryer, one who values continual growth.

Transparent self *vs.* Opaque self—The honest, real self is very important to the life-seeker. Little energy is expended in maintaining a role or a facade. This does not mean a person is tactless or crude, rather he has a healthy self-concept and feels he can love and be loved as he is.

Self-controlled *vs.* Other-controlled—This relates not to self-sufficiency, for the life-seeking person is extremely dependent on others, but to the motivation in one's life. When a facade is necessary and a person cannot be himself, control by others is strong. The life-seeking person responds to an inner motivation and acts by choice based on personal commitments.

Present-oriented *vs.* Past/Future-oriented—Rather than treasuring the good old days or living for the future, this quality relates to the activity of a person as he is and where he is now; there is no escape to another time or place. For the life-seeker, the past is a servant of the present—providing valuable insights into understanding and coping with present experience—and the future will be a child of the present. What happens now is life; all that was or will be, if dwelled upon, becomes an escape from reality.

Transforming *vs.* Preserving—Here, again, the emphasis is not on a choice between transforming or preserving. Rather the decision must be made in terms of priority: are we to focus most of our resources on receiving, conserving, and preserving everything that exists; or are we to evaluate what exists and, based on our commitments, seek to transform that which may not be acceptable. Perhaps the best example of this is given by David Hunter in his near classic *Christian Education as Engagement:* Are we called to preserve our culture as we receive it, or do we seek to transform it in light of Christian beliefs?

Emotionally honest *vs.* Overly rational—The life-seeking person responds to head and to heart, to reasoning and to feeling. Both responses, as long as they are honest, represent variables that significantly influence life, and thus learning and growing. There is little effort made to rationalize or to explain away feelings or actions which may be based on feelings. An honest want or desire does not have to be explained rationally. It simply exists.

Means consonant with ends *vs.* Ends justify means—The process or means, used in achieving an end is quite often the most influential factor in determining a person's attitude and commitment toward that end. Thus the means and the end make the whole. Anything achieved by a person or organization changes those involved. And the greatest influence on these people is not the product but the way in which the product is produced. Thus the life-seeking leader cannot separate a desired end from the means that are necessary to achieve it; the growth of people must be an integral part of accomplishing any goal.

Lifelong learning *vs.* Formal education—Every experience can be an opportunity for learning. A person need not depend solely on the systematic, graded approach to education generally offered in a classroom. Reflection on spontaneous or unstructured activities and feelings, informal inquiry growing out of personal interest, and problem solving through trial and error are some of the opportunities for growth that are available throughout life. Obviously we all continue learning regardless of our orientation in this area. But the life-seeking person generally perceives all experience as opportunity for learning and growing; thus his expectations often enable him to gain or improve knowledge, attitudes, and skills when others may perceive nothing of value. Thus it is fairly evident that the life seeker places great value on the process of learning instead of simply stressing the study of subjects.

The life seeker does not reject the content of formalized education. Rather he uses it in service to the present and in preparation for the future. Added to content however must be a process of learning where the development of problem-solving skills and of personal values is dominant. Using education in achieving a satisfying and meaningful life under any combination of circumstances is the desired goal.

"Want" commitment *vs.* "Ought" commitment—This characteristic grows out of a basic tension in every person between developing one's own values and accepting the values of others. Values may not be consciously derived from others, for their incorporation is primarily due to the permeating influence of significant persons experienced since birth. The tension begins when a person begins to examine these passed-down values in light of his present experience and finds discrepancies. At this point the person can either avoid reality and seek to reinforce presently-held values, or he can begin the process of adjusting his value system so that it is congruent with his experience.

Basically, the life-seeking person feels free to evaluate and make his own commitments; he tends to avoid operating out of "oughtness" which indicates that one is controlled by outside forces.

As a Christian, the life seeker is one who has consciously struggled with and developed personal convictions concerning his relationship to Jesus Christ. Rather than accepting religious convictions secondhand or simply affirming parental commitments, he appraises his world and comes up with values and beliefs for which he can stand without being motivated by guilt feelings.

These are some of the features that create the image of a growing person, one committed to seeking an ever-increasing maturity in Jesus Christ.

No one feature stands alone; all are interconnected, and success or failure in one area affects the others. Even so, the basic expectation of life-seeking persons is that the overall direction of personal and spiritual growth is toward life and away from a sequestered or dormant existence.

Relationship Between Environment and Personal Qualities

The relationship between the environment in which one lives and personal qualities that are developed is something like the proverbial question about which came first, the chicken or the egg. One's environment is the greatest influence on the development of life-seeking qualities. But it is a commitment to life-seeking values by a community of people that creates such an environment.

As a person practices life-seeking behavior, it is the response of persons who are significant to him that either encourages or discourages similar actions in the future. For example, if a person tries something and fails, there is a great deal of difference between a supportive, encouraging environment and one that conveys an I-told-you-so reaction.

The environment or community that values *trying* encourages life-seeking behavior. When a person succeeds, there is not only praise and recognition but also support and encouragement for continued growth. The general pattern is not so much to recognize success as an end in itself; rather success is valued as a stepping-stone in the growth process.

When success is incomplete or failure occurs, the environmental support and encouragement increases rather than diminishes, and the community helps those who are involved focus on reflection. This is for the purpose of examining feelings, understanding motives, evaluating actions, and determining the learning gained simply because of being involved in the experience.

Thus both the content of learning and the process through which one acquires that content provide opportunities for growth. And it is the environment in which people live that develops within them a grow or no-grow attitude toward these opportunities.

Basic Beliefs and Personal Values

Behind the environment and personal qualities that elicit growth are certain beliefs that in essence are the foundation for life-giving leadership.

Basic to all beliefs and values is a commitment to a God-given and sustained creation. All that was, is, and will be is of God and has purpose in the ultimate intent, design, and direction of the universe. This is not to imply that creation is a past accomplishment; rather creation is as ongoing and alive as is the Creator.

The second belief relates to man. Life-giving leadership acknowledges along with the Scriptures that man is God's highest creation. Man, rather than being innately sinful and worthless, is seen as basically good and of ultimate value to a loving God. Instead of needing to be limited, controlled, and manipulated in order to achieve the purposes of God, man can most effectively serve when his potential is released and subsequent actions are self-directed based on personal convictions.

Life-giving leadership does not, however, ignore the reality of sin. The belief is that sin is not necessary but that, in the course of life, is inevitable. Neither sin nor salvation can be passed down or received from others; thus great value is placed on each person entering into a personal saving and forgiving relationship with Jesus Christ.

A third belief is that Christian growth is primarily experiential and instrumental. Knowing about something is a very elementary level of learning and provides little adaptive or coping potential for a person. Basically, knowing about implies little more than the ability to recall information. Life-giving leadership goes beyond this to point to the interaction of a person with that which he is learning. The knowledge, skills, and attitudes acquired in any growth or learning experience are all interrelated and each affects the others. Instead of dealing simply with knowledge such as that which can be verified by scientific observation or measurement, life-giving leadership holds that learning in its natural state occurs when a person is experiencing and reflecting on normal, day-to-day activities.

Not only must Christian growth be experiential but it must also be instrumental. That is it must be related to and assist the learner in achieving or progressing toward goals to which he is committed.

People, unless pressured, naturally pursue activities that help them achieve goals to which they are committed. When learning is instrumental, it helps you to achieve something. And this is the normal pattern of growth and development throughout life.

Life-giving leadership does not, however, arbitrarily reject experiences that may not be perceived as instrumental. There are many areas of learning that the community in which one lives has found to be of value and thus wishes for him to appropriate. This is a valid constraint on an individual's natural motivation for learning, since a people to a great extent are what they find of value and pass on from generation to generation. Especially is this true of the followers of Jesus Christ. This is not to imply, however, that manipulative and coercive approaches to leadership are condoned. Learning experiences can still be designed to reinforce individual worth and to elicit natural motivation and personal involvement.

Obviously there could be many complementing beliefs growing out of these three mentioned, but they would vary greatly from person to person. These three represent the common ground among life-giving leadership and, in general, are the strongest influences on all other beliefs and practices.

Personal values inherent in life-giving leaders cannot easily be catalogued and presented as an ideal for which to strive. What I have done is to present some general values and to show the practical consequences that flow from them. Different persons would rank these values differently.

Instead of describing that which a life-giving leader might believe, let me close in a more life-giving way with a process-oriented statement concerning values: The values assumed by life-giving leaders grow out of basic beliefs and are developed by each person as he interacts with his environment. The values held are personal but not private; they are publicly affirmed in all life and acted on with consistency. Values grow out of an examination of possibilities; and commitments, when they are made, are freely given.

The life-giving leader not only cherishes his values but he also lives them and, in essence, develops a life-style that exemplifies what he values. This then is what life-giving leadership is all about: believing, practicing, and incarnating a leadership life-style developed not by man but by God in Christ.

"In him was life, and the life was the light of men" (John 1:4, RSV).

Resources

Bell, Gerald D. *The Achievers.* Chapel Hill, North Carolina: Preston-Hill, 1973.

Blake, Robert R. and Mouton, Jane S. *The Managerial Grid.* Houston: Gulf Publishing, 1964.

Clemmons, William and Hester, Harvey. *Growth Through Groups.* Nashville: Broadman Press, 1974.

Collins, Gary R. *Man in Motion: the Psychology of Human Motivation.* Carol Stream, Illinois: Creation House, 1973.

Dow, Robert A. *Learning Through Encounter.* Valley Forge: Judson Press, 1971.

Dunnam, Maxie D., et. al. *The Manipulator and the Church.* Nashville: Abingdon Press, 1968.

Edge, Findley B. *The Greening of the Church.* Waco: Word Books, 1971.

Gangel, Kenneth O. *Competent to Lead.* Chicago: Moody Press, 1974.

Glasse, James D. *Putting It Together in the Parish.* Nashville: Abingdon Press, 1973.

Goble, Frank G. *The Third Force: The Psychology of Abraham Maslow* New York: Grossman Publishers, 1970.

Harris, Thomas A. *I'm OK—You're OK.* New York: Harper and Row, 1967.

Hendrix, John and Householder, Lloyd (eds.). *The Equipping of Disciples.* Nashville: Broadman Press, 1977.

Hendrix, John D., et. al. *Nexus: Discovering Spiritual Gifts.* Nashville: Convention Press, 1974.

Hersey, Paul and Blanchard, Kenneth H. *Management of Organizational Behavior.* Englewood Cliffs: Prentice-Hall, 1972.

Howe, Reuel L. *Survival Plus.* New York: Seabury Press, 1971.

Hunter, David R. *Christian Education as Engagement.* New York: Seabury Press, 1963.

Jourard, Sidney M. *The Transparent Self.* New York: Van Nostrand Reinhold, 1971.

Knowles, Malcolm. *Self-Directed Learning.* New York: Association Press, 1975.

Lesly, Philip. *The People Factor: Managing the Human Climate.* Homewood, Illinois: Dow Jones-Irwin, 1974.

Leypoldt, Martha M. *Learning Is Change.* Valley Forge: Judson Press, 1971.

Likert, Rensis. *New Patterns of Management.* New York: McGraw-Hill, 1961.

McDonough, Reginald M. *Working with Volunteer Leaders in the Church.* Nashville: Broadman Press, 1976.

McGregor, Douglas. *The Human Side of Enterprise.* New York: McGraw-Hill, 1960.

Maslow, Abraham H. *Motivation and Personality.* New York: Harper and Row, 1954.

O'Connor, Elizabeth. *Eighth Day of Creation.* Waco: Word Books, 1971.

_____. *Journey Inward, Journey Outward.* New York: Harper & Row, 1968.

O'Neill, George and O'Neill, Nina. *Shifting Gears: Finding Security in a Changing World.* New York: A. M. Evans, 1967.

Rogillio, Byron Lee. *How the Spiritual Gifts of the Laos Can Be Called Forth, Developed, and Utilized in the Local Church.* Ann Arbor: University Microfilms, 1971.

Rouch, Mark. *Competent Ministry.* Nashville: Abingdon Press, 1974.

Schaller, Lyle E. *The Change Agent.* Nashville: Abingdon Press, 1972.

_____. *The Decision-Makers.* Nashville: Abingdon Press, 1974.

Sedwick, Robert C. *Interaction.* Englewood Cliffs: Prentice-Hall, 1974.

Sherrill, Lewis J. *The Gift of Power.* New York: Macmillan, 1955.

Sperry, Len, et. al. *You Can Make It Happen: A Guide to Self-Actualization and Organizational Change.* Reading, Massachusetts: Addison-Wesley, 1977.

Stagg, Frank. *The Holy Spirit Today.* Nashville: Broadman Press, 1974.

Stedman, Ray C. *Body Life.* Glendale, California: Regal Books, 1972.

Toffler, Alvin M. *Future Shock.* New York: Random House, 1970.

Tournier, Paul. *A Place for You.* London: SCM Press, 1968.